W9-DGI-701

A Great
and
Sublime Fool

the story of

MARK TWAIN

A Great
and
Sublime Fool

the story of

MARK TWAIN

Peggy Caravantes

MORGAN
REYNOLDS

PUBLISHING

Greensboro, North Carolina

WORLD WRITERS

Charles Dickens

Jane Austen

Ralph Ellison

Stephen King

Robert Frost

O. Henry

Roald Dahl

Jonathan Swift

Leo Tolstoy

Zora Neale Hurston

Mark Twain

Mary Shelley

A GREAT AND SUBLIME FOOL:
THE STORY OF MARK TWAIN
Copyright © 2009 By Peggy Caravantes

Caravantes, Peggy, 1935-
A great and sublime fool : the story of Mark Twain / by Peggy Caravantes.
-- 1st ed.
    p. cm.
Includes bibliographical references (p.   ) and index.
ISBN-13: 978-1-59935-088-2
ISBN-10: 1-59935-088-2
1. Twain, Mark, 1835-1910--Juvenile literature. 2. Authors, American--19th
century--Biography--Juvenile literature. 3. Humorists, American--19th cen-
tury--Biography--Juvenile literature. 4. Journalists--United States--Biography-
-Juvenile literature. I. Title.
PS1331.C29 2010
818'.408--dc22
[B]
                                                2008034139

Printed in the United States of America
First Edition

Appreciation to my sister Dorothy Featherling
for her support and editing skills

"Ah, well, I am a great and sublime fool. But then I am God's fool, and all his works must be contemplated with respect."

—Mark Twain
Letter to W. D. Howells, 1877

Contents

ONE:
Family Ties...11

TWO:
Apprenticeship... 25

THREE:
Traveler... 41

FOUR:
Courtship and Marriage..63

FIVE:
Author and Investor 83

SIX:
Financial Struggles 104

SEVEN:
Troubling Times...122

EIGHT:
Halley's Comet Comes Again 141

Timeline 155
Sources 161
Bibliography...170
Web Sites 173
Index 174

Mark Twain *(Library of Congress)*

 10

Family Ties

As a child, Sam Clemens sat for hours watching the activity on the Mississippi River, listening to the waves lapping against the wharf, and daydreaming. He dreamed of becoming a riverboat pilot: to Sam, a pilot was the only "unfettered and entirely independent human being that lived on the earth." One day, desperate for that freedom, Sam slipped aboard a docked riverboat. When the steamboat edged out of the harbor, Sam crept out of his hiding place to watch the water and the passing scenery. Suddenly, a downpour soaked him, and he scrambled to get back into his hiding place. He was not completely successful, and a crew member saw Sam's legs sticking out. The Captain put Sam ashore at the boat's next stop in the town of Louisiana, Missouri, where some of his mother's relatives lived. They took Sam home, where his father punished him for running away. But the desire for freedom, and for an escape never left him.

Samuel Langhorne Clemens was born on November 30, 1835, as Halley's Comet neared the end of its streak across the sky. He arrived in the world in a two-room frame house in Florida, Missouri, a two-street village less than two hundred miles from Indian territory. Sickly and frail, Sammy was mostly bedridden until he was four years old. He was the third son of John Marshall Clemens and Jane Lampton Clemens, both Southerners. John Marshall came from Virginia, where he was a minor slaveholder with three inherited slaves. Marshall had become head of his family's household at the age of seven when his father was accidentally killed while helping a neighbor build a house.

Halley's Comet shone bright in the sky when Samuel Clemens was born in 1835. (*Courtesy of NASA*)

An unidentified man standing in front of the house where Clemens was born in Florida, Missouri. *(Library of Congress)*

The Clemenses later moved to Kentucky, where Marshall met and married Jane Lampton. Jane was beautiful and witty, and she attended church regularly. From his mother Sam inherited curly red hair, a delicate complexion, drawling speech, and small, shapely hands and feet. Hating the curls and thinking them effeminate, he plastered them to his skull with water. As he grew older, Sam enjoyed his mother's natural wit.

Jane's vivacious personality was a contrast to that of her husband, who rarely smiled and never laughed. With his tall, lean build and piercing gray eyes, he looked like a Puritan, and acted like one as well. A hard-working man, Marshall Clemens seldom spoke to his children and never showed them any affection. As an adult, Sam recalled that the two were never close: "My father and I were always on the most distant terms when I was a boy—a sort of armed neutrality so to speak."

Prior to her accepting Marshall's proposal, Jane had been courted for two years by a young doctor named Richard Barrett. Finally, he made plans to propose to her, but the arrangements for their meeting became confused. When Jane did not come to the appointed place, Barrett thought she had rejected him and left town.

Irritated, Jane accepted John Marshall Clemens' proposal and demanded they marry immediately. The wedding took place on May 6, 1823. Marshall was twenty-five; Jane, twenty. She remained a loyal wife to him, but many years later Sam wrote about them: "All through my boyhood I had noticed that the attitude of my father and mother toward each other was that of courteous, considerate and always respectful, and even deferential, friends; that they were always kind toward each other, but that there was nothing warmer; there were no outward and visible demonstrations of affection."

After the couple married, they lived in Gainsborough, Tennessee, where their first child, a son named Orion, was born on July 17, 1825. Marshall faced problems almost immediately—poor health brought on by his studying late at night to become a lawyer, lack of clients for legal work, and only a small success with the general store he opened. Over the next several years, the family moved frequently, always seeking a more stable financial situation. Hoping to improve his family's fortune, Marshall started buying land grants. Eventually, he purchased 75,000 acres of Tennessee land, all for less than five hundred dollars. As he one day surveyed the property, he assured himself: "Whatever befalls me now, my heirs are secure. I may not live to see these acres turn into silver and gold, but my children will."

However, over time the land became more of a curse than a blessing. In later years, Marshall Clemens' dream of wealth from the land appeared in the plot of his son's novel, *The Gilded Age*, when Squire Hawkins tells his wife Nancy that he has taken care of their children: "I've looked out for *them*, Nancy . . . Do you see these papers? Well, they are evidence that I have taken up Seventy-five Thousand Acres of Land in this county—think what an enormous fortune it will be some day! . . . the whole tract would not sell for over a third of a cent an acre now, but some day people will; be glad to get it for . . . *a thousand dollars an acre!*"

Two daughters soon joined the Clemens household— Pamela in 1827 and Margaret in 1830. A son, Pleasant Hannibal, born in 1828, lived only three months. Another son, Benjamin, was born in 1832. With more children to support, his business failing, and his health still poor, Marshall eagerly accepted an invitation from his brother-in-law John Quarles to join him and his family in Missouri in a town named Florida. The chance to make a new start after having had his credit wiped out in the national financial crisis of 1834 appealed to Marshall. Jane further encouraged the move so that she could live nearer to her favorite sister Patsy, Quarles's wife. Although Marshall sold what little they still owned, he kept the 75,000 acres of land.

The Clemens family started out in the spring of 1835 and in June reached Florida, located at the fork of the Salt River.

At that time Florida had no direct connection to the outside world, but the current residents occupying the town's twenty-one houses hoped that someday the Salt River could become navigable enough to allow access to the great Mississippi River. When the family arrived in Florida, Jane was pregnant again, although she did not know it at the time. Six months later her third son Samuel was born two months prematurely. Jane worried that she would lose this sickly son also.

For some time Sam wavered between life and death. On the occasions when his health improved, he entertained the family. Noticing that all the household pets had tails, Sam wondered where his tail was. He complained to one of his uncles: "The dog has a tail bebind, the cat has a tail bebind, and I haven't any tail bebind at all at all." To Sam's great satisfaction, the uncle made a tail of paper and pinned it on Sam's white dress.

At first Marshall worked with his brother-in-law at Quarles's general merchandise store. About a year later he opened his own store and made his oldest son, eleven-year-old Orion, the clerk. But what Marshall really wanted to do was practice law. He knew though that more people needed to come to Florida if he were to get enough clients to earn a living. Again Marshall began buying land. He believed that once the Salt River became a link to the Mississippi, more settlers would come and he could sell the land at a profit. However, another financial panic in 1837 removed any chance for that passage. Already talk had turned to railroads as the next merchandise carriers to the great river. Marshall had once again put his money in the wrong place.

Henry, the last of the seven children born to the Clemenses, arrived in 1838—another child to support on a diminishing income. Marshall realized he needed to move his family again. In February 1839 he saw an ad that cheap property was available in Hannibal, Missouri, a village forty miles eastward between two bluffs overlooking the Mississippi River. Marshall started trying to accumulate enough money to buy property in Hannibal.

On August 17, before the family left Florida, they suffered the death of their nine-year-old daughter Margaret from bilious fever, a viral infection of the liver. Jane became extremely distraught at the loss of a second child. However, Marshall plodded on with his plans to move. Just a couple of weeks before Sam's fourth birthday, Marshall sold some of the Florida land in order to buy a city block in Hannibal, a town that already boasted one thousand residents. In November the family left Florida for the trip to Hannibal. Orion (age fourteen), Pamela (twelve), Benjamin (seven), Sam (four), Henry (sixteen months) and their slave Jenny joined Marshall and Jane in the move.

Their first home in Hannibal was the Virginia House, a dilapidated hotel on the property Marshall had purchased. From the hotel they could watch the Mississippi River flowing less than fifty yards away. The family settled on the second floor with plans to rent the rooms on the first floor. Again Marshall opened a general store stocked with goods he purchased using a $2,000 loan. He put the now fifteen-year-old Orion in charge of the store as a clerk. Between Orion's daydreaming, the debt already incurred to stock the store, and a shortage of customers, the store did not flourish. As it floundered, Marshall borrowed more money and tried to get some legal business.

Sam sensed his parents' anxiety about finances and began to have nightmares and convulsions. At night he became a sleepwalker. All of these problems led to Sam frequently running away and getting into more mischief than all of his brothers and sisters combined. In his mother's old age, Sam inquired of her:

> I suppose that during all that time you were uneasy about me?"
>
> Yes, the whole time.
>
> Afraid I wouldn't live?
>
> . . . No—afraid you would.

Shortly before his fifth birthday, the family decided to send Sam to school. His mother wanted him out of the house and told anyone who listened: "He drives me crazy with his didoes, when he is in the house, and when he is out of it I am expecting every minute that some one will bring him home half dead."

Since Missouri had no public schools, his mother enrolled him in a "dame school," a concept patterned after similar British schools in which housewives taught young children in their homes. The teacher, Elizabeth Horr, charged twenty-five cents per week for each of her students whom she instructed in a small log house on Main Street. She taught the children good manners, geography, spelling, reading, and long division. However, morality was at the center of the curriculum, and Mrs. Horr always began the day with a prayer and the reading of a New Testament chapter, followed by her explanation of the text and the rule for behavior it suggested. A concept that she often repeated was "ask and ye shall receive."

When Sam saw that Margaret Kooneman, the baker's daughter, brought a gingerbread to school each day, he decided to test what Mrs. Horr said. The next morning during prayer time, Sam pleaded with God for gingerbread. When Sam opened his eyes, he noticed that Margaret's gingerbread was in plain view and within easy reach. As she looked the other way, Sam plucked it from her desk. Although he was disappointed in the following days when the prayer never worked again, he later reminisced, "In all my life I believe I never enjoyed an answer to a prayer more than I enjoyed that one."

With his mother too busy to supervise any but the youngest children, Sam enjoyed life without restraints. Although he had been a sickly child, by the time he was seven he had developed into an active, wiry boy. With a group of boys his own age, Sam organized a gang and became the self-appointed leader. Assisting him in all their adventures was six-year-old Will Bowen, Sam's best friend.

One of their escapades proved almost deadly. A favorite place of Sam's was Holliday's Hill, and he and Will spent many hours at its peak. Each time they went there they worked at trying to nudge a huge boulder, hoping to send it hurtling down the hill. One afternoon they spent three hours with their shoulders against the giant rock and pushed hard. Suddenly, the boulder loosened and raced down the hill, demolishing everything in its path. A cart driver and his mule came into view just as the boulder neared the bottom of the hill. Fortunately, for the driver, at the last minute the rock hit a hard object, causing the boulder to fly over the driver's head. The huge rock crashed into the shop of a man who made wooden casks and tubs. Sam retold this episode in *Innocents Abroad*, where he concludes: "Then we said it was perfectly magnificent and left. Because the coopers [workers] were starting up the hill to inquire." Sam and Will escaped before the adults reached the top of the hill.

Sam's father had little time to supervise his children because of his work, his financial problems, and his poor health, possibly tuberculosis for which he ordered cases of a dark medicine whose side effects may have been worse than his disease. Although he spent little time with the children, he did care about their education and bought books when he could afford them and also subscribed to the premiere children's magazine of the day, *Parley's Magazine*. But in later years, reflecting upon his childhood relationship with his father, Sam said, "My own knowledge of him amounted to little more than an introduction."

Because he yearned for a genial father figure, Sam turned to his Uncle John Quarles, who owned a farm outside Hannibal. Sam spent two to three months of every summer in the place—he considered it a paradise. During the day he waded in chilly brooks, climbed trees, and picked ripe fruit. Meals were banquets featuring fried chicken, roast pig, venison, squirrel, and rabbit. In addition to the meats there were hot biscuits, pancakes, corn-on-the-cob, sweet potatoes, watermelons, and cantaloupes. Apples and peaches found their way into cobblers and pies.

When the sun went down, Sam and his cousins went to the slave quarters, where Sam developed a fondness for the black servants. In reminiscing in later years, he said: "It was on the farm that I got my strong liking for . . . [the black] race and my appreciation of certain of its fine qualities." One of the children's favorites was Aunt Hannah, rumored to be one thousand years old. According to the other slaves, Aunt

Clemens spent most of his childhood on the Mississippi River. (*Library of Congress*)

Hannah had seen the exodus of the Israelites from Egypt and had talked to Moses. As she watched the Pharoah drown, her white hair had thinned to almost baldness.

Sam especially enjoyed the songs and stories told when the slaves and the children gathered around the open fireplace. A tale that never failed to mesmerize Sam was Uncle Ned's story of the golden arm. The story concerned a man who had a wife with an arm of pure gold. Then she died and was buried in the cemetery. One night her husband went to her grave, dug up her body, and cut off the golden arm. Shortly thereafter, a ghost that looked like his wife appeared to him. The ghost repeatedly asked, "W-h-a-r-r's my golden arm?"

Each time Uncle Ned asked the question, he stared into the eyes of a different child. Holding his hands in front of him like claws, he moved closer to the shivering children. He uttered the question in a ghost-like voice, pausing dramatically before moving to the next child. All of a sudden he pounced on one of the children, shook the child's shoulders, and shouted: "You've got it!" The frightened child looked over his shoulder as Uncle Ned finished the story with "*and she tore him all to pieces!*" Having heard the story numerous times in his childhood, Sam learned the value of a pause in storytelling. Such dramatic pauses became a characteristic of his public storytelling years later.

The death of Sam's ten-year-old brother Benjamin clouded the carefree days on the farm. Ben became ill and died all within a week's time. The death of another child came as a harsh emotional blow to Sam's parents, especially his mother, who mourned loudly for days after the burial of her third child. Jane made each of the remaining children touch the cheek of their dead brother "to make them understand the calamity that had befallen." Sam never forgot the incident and began a practice that lasted a lifetime: blaming himself for events over which he had no control.

Benjamin's death prompted Jane's return to attending church, taking all four children, even though her husband Marshall refused to go with them. Jane selected a strict Presbyterian denomination. According to her church's doctrine, God doomed all sinners to hell, and only he chose who would be saved. Sensitive little Sam listened to this dire prediction Sunday after Sunday, instilling a fear that unless he was one of the elect, he had no chance of avoiding the fiery depths of hell. However, the church preached that everyone should lead a moral life just in case he was one of the chosen, leading Sam, many years later to write in his notebook:

"If Christ were here now, There is one thing he would not be—a Christian."

The preacher claimed Satan was real and visited Hannibal often, which interested Sam. When he questioned his Sunday school teacher about Satan, she scolded him for "inquiring into matters above my age and comprehension." From the pulpit Sam also heard that God approved of slavery, "that it was a holy thing, and that the doubter need only look in the Bible if he wished to settle his mind." Thus, as a boy Sam never realized that slavery was wrong. He regarded all blacks as his friends and played with the black children who were his age. However, even at that young age, Sam sensed subtle differences. He later wrote: "We were comrades and yet not comrades; color and condition interposed a subtle line which both parties were conscious of and which rendered complete fusion impossible."

The difference between his own life and that of Sandy, a young slave boy who worked in the Clemens household, was impressed upon Sam's mind after he complained to his mother that Sandy made too much noise. The constant noise irritated Sam one day, and he rushed to his mother to complain about Sandy's singing. He begged his mother to make Sandy be quiet. As tears filled her eyes, Jane responded to her son: "Poor thing, when he sings it shows that he is not remembering, and that comforts me; but when he is still I am afraid he is thinking, and I cannot bear it. He will never see his mother again; if he can sing, I must not hinder it, but be thankful for it. If you were older, you would understand me; then the friendless child's noise would make you glad."

Although by this time, Sam's father Marshall had become appointed justice of the peace, the slim salary did not provide

Mark Twain's home museum in Hannibal, Missouri *(Courtesy of Dennis MacDonald/Alamy)*

for all the Clemens family. Marshall sent his oldest son Orion to St. Louis to become a printer's apprentice. This decision was a blow to Orion's hopes and dreams of becoming a professional man some day—a lifestyle he believed appropriate for a judge's son and an heir to the Tennessee land. Printing was a trade and a step down the social ladder.

To support the family while Marshall tried to get some legal work, Jane took in a few boarders. Meanwhile, Marshall earned the respect of the townspeople for his civic work, and the situation gradually improved. He eventually built a house on some land given to him by a cousin. The family's move into this house in 1844 marked the beginning of the boyhood Sam would later depict in *The Adventures of Tom Sawyer*.

TWO

Apprenticeship

Sam, now a healthy nine-year-old, roamed freely around Hannibal. For the first time, he began to notice the cruel and brutal manner in which people treated slaves. This bothered him so much that he often had trouble sleeping. To him, the violence he observed toward the slaves was a warning of the punishment he could expect when he died if he did not lead a better life. Whenever there was a thunderstorm, he cowered in his bed, believing God was threatening him.

Sam had many hours of fun though as he roamed hills and woods and explored caves. He finally learned to swim after almost drowning in Bear Creek twice and six times more in the Mississippi River. Each time someone was there to pull him out. He later joked: "I do not now know who the people were who interfered with the intentions of a Providence wiser than themselves, but I hold a grudge against them yet."

One escapade, when Sam was ten years old, nearly killed him. A measles epidemic spread quickly through Hannibal, killing at least one youngster almost every day. Jane Clemens panicked, fearing she might lose another child. She did everything she could to prevent her family from getting the measles, including confining Sam and his siblings to their house. Accustomed to freely roaming Hannibal and unable to tolerate his mother's hovering, Sam decided to take matters into his own hands. He would expose himself to the measles and either live or die.

Sam sneaked into the house of his best friend Will Bowen, who was confined to a second-floor bedroom with the measles. Sam crawled into bed with Will and lay there until Will's mother discovered him. She immediately sent Sam home but within a few days, he managed to sneak back into Will's bed. By that time his young friend was too sick even to know Sam was there. Sam succeeded in getting the measles and, for two weeks, hovered between life and death. The doctor gave up hope of saving Sam, and his tearful family gathered around the boy's bed. Then the doctor decided to try an old-fashioned treatment. He put small sacks of hot ashes all over Sam, hoping to sweat the disease out of the boy's body. The unusual remedy worked, and Sam soon recovered.

Sam attended Mr. Dawson's upper-level school for students ranging in ages from twelve to young adult. However, the young Sam was not an eager student and looked forward to escaping school to roam around Hannibal. One day after playing hooky, Sam did not want to return home and face his punishment. He decided to spend the night in his father's office. He did not know, however, that a man had been stabbed to death that day and the corpse laid on the floor of

the judge's quarters. Sam later described the frightening discovery in *Innocents Abroad*: "a long, dusky, shapeless thing
stretched upon the floor. . . . A white human hand lay in the
moonlight! . . . the pallid face of a man was there, with the
corners of his mouth drawn down, and the eyes fixed and
glassy in death!"

Sam ignored most admonitions from his parents, including their warning against smoking. In a place where tobacco
fields flourished, Sam had his choice of cigars at ten cents or
smoking an inexpensive corncob pipe. Chewing tobacco was
almost free. This easy availability made smoking and chewing common among all ages and genders. Although preachers
warned against it on moral grounds, no one knew that it was
a health risk, and the only abstinence rule was "never smoke
more than one cigar at a time."

Another influence in Sam's life was his friendship with
Tom Blankenship, the village drunkard's son. Sam and
his gang envied Tom, who did not have to follow the rules
expected of them. Tom did not have to bathe, wear clean
clothes, or go to school or church regularly. He stole most of
his food, although he was a good hunter and fisherman. "He
was the only really independent person—boy or man—in the
community, and by consequence he was tranquilly and con-
tinuously happy." When Sam became a novelist, Tom became
the model for the character of Huckleberry Finn.

Sam's boyhood freedom ended abruptly at the age of
twelve when his father died. By that time Marshall had
declared bankruptcy, after a friend failed to pay a loan that
Marshall cosigned. In November 1846 Marshall made plans
to seek election to become a circuit court clerk, a position
that would have paid him a small but steady salary. Since

the election was not until August 1847, Marshall decided to campaign in the county seat the February prior to the election. However, he got caught in bad weather while making the trip, and the exposure to cold, wet conditions brought on.pneumonia. Just before he died, Marshall urged the family to hold on to the Tennessee land, believing that he was leaving them a grand legacy. "Cling to the land, and wait. Let nothing beguile it away from you," he begged. Then he kissed nineteen-year-old Pamela but said nothing to his wife and other children before dying on March 24, 1847, at the age of forty-nine.

Jane saw that Sam was deeply affected by his father's death, and she decided to use his grief as an opportunity to extract a promise of better behavior from her son. She took Sam by the hand and led him to his father's coffin, where she told him that she had a serious request for him. The sobbing boy replied, "Oh mother, I will do anything, anything you ask of me except go to school; I can't do that!" Since that was exactly what Jane had planned to ask of Sam, she talked to him about an alternative so that he would not just be running wild. Sam and she agreed that in the near future he would become an apprentice and learn the printing trade.

Twenty-one-year-old Orion now had the responsibility of caring for the family—a burden he was not capable of assuming. In St. Louis, Orion earned $10 a month as a printer. He sent $3 to his mother, who was not much help as she drew more inward, absorbed in omens and dreams. She became obsessed with the color red and would have worn it all the time if her family had not objected. Jane started smoking a pipe, playing cards, and adopting cats. Although sister Pamela instructed a few music students, her main task was caring for their mother. Sam and Henry still attended school,

A young boy working as a printer's apprentice. Clemens learned much about the formation and organization of words during his years working in a print shop. *(Library of Congress)*

although Jane urged Sam to find after-school work wherever he could.

Sam found a job as a paperboy, and one of the headlines that he got to shout about was the United States' victory at Chapultepec Castle that turned the tide in the U.S.-Mexican War. The officer who led the charge by having a howitzer lifted into a church bell tower was Ulysses S. Grant, whose memoirs Sam would one day publish.

The battle of Chapultepec Castle during the U.S.-Mexican War. *(Library of Congress)*

In June 1848, Jane, according to their agreement, apprenticed Sam to the *Gazette*, which was soon purchased by Joseph P. Ament, who changed the paper's name to the *Courier*. As an apprentice Sam went to get water, swept the floors, and put logs in the fireplace. As was typical for apprentices, he received no salary. He was entitled to two suits every year, but instead of new ones, Sam received Ament's hand-me-downs. The other boys ridiculed Sam dressed in Ament's much-too-large clothes. Ament provided Sam's meals and allowed him to sleep at night on the print shop floor.

Although Sam hated Ament, he did learn from him how to set type, a tedious, repetitive job. From a case of metal typeface cast backwards and arranged alphabetically, Sam had to select individual letters to make words that fit into metal sticks. Sam became quite adept at typesetting.

Furthermore, his work typesetting engendered in him an interest in history and literature. In later years he commented: "One isn't a printer ten years without setting up acres of good and bad literature, and learning—unconsciously at first, consciously later—to discriminate between the two." Sam developed a deeper interest in history when he picked up in the street a page from a book about Joan of Arc. Sam had never heard her story; once he started reading about the Maid of Orleans, he felt great compassion for her as well as hatred for her persecutors. The interest in medieval times that began with a single page developed over much of his life and resulted in *Personal Recollections of Joan of Arc* in 1896.

Excitement hummed in Hannibal in 1849 as fortune hunters swept through the village on their way to the California Gold Rush. Sam and his friends yearned to join the stream of prospectors, nicknamed the 49ers. To Sam, travel represented adventure and glory. He sought another form of glory by joining the Cadets of Temperance, a national organization dedicated to a "no smoking" pledge. Membership allowed Sam to have a coveted red sash and to wear it in May Day and Fourth of July parades. After he had marched in each of these parades in 1850, he quit the Cadets and resumed smoking.

That same year Orion returned to Hannibal and started his own weekly newspaper, the *Western Union*. The following year he borrowed $500 to buy the *Journal* and merged the two papers. Sam went to work for his brother as a printer, and their younger brother Henry became an apprentice. Although the paper struggled financially and Sam did not always get

Joan of Arc (*Library of Congress*)

paid his salary, the three years he spent there were important to Sam as a writer because he first saw his words in print and found that he enjoyed being a humorist.

Sam first realized his ability to tell a humorous story when he shared with friends the story of Jim Wolf, a co-worker, who at Sam's urging had tried to drive away cats fighting outside Jim's window one night. Jim climbed out on the roof, wearing only socks and a nightshirt, just as Sam's sister Pamela

The earliest known photograph of Clemens, at age fifteen. *(Courtesy of The Granger Collection, New York)*

and some of her friends came outside to cool plates of candy they had made. Startled by the appearance of the girls, Jim slipped and fell right into fourteen plates of hot candy. The next day Sam gleefully told the story to a friend who could not stop laughing, and Sam realized for the first time that he had a gift for humorous stories.

A year later he tried something similar in writing when Orion again went to Tennessee to try to sell some of their land because finances were so tight for the Clemens family. While he was gone, Orion gave Sam the responsibility of publishing at least one issue of the *Journal*. Believing his brother's paper was dull, Sam decided to make it more entertaining. He began by writing an article mocking a warning that appeared in a rival paper, the *Tri-Weekly Messenger*— that citizens should beware of mad dogs. As he would do frequently in the years to come, Sam assumed another name—Dog-be-deviled Citizen— to mockingly suggest getting rid of all dogs. Higgins, the other editor, fired back a response and the volley of exchanges continued to the point of becoming personal.

Higgins was trying to recover from an unsuccessful love affair, and his emotions were raw. The attack by Sam sent Higgins over the edge, and he started to commit suicide by drowning himself. At the last minute he lost the courage to do so, resulting in Sam's putting in the *Journal* a picture depicting Higgins with a doglike head wading into the water, holding a lantern in one hand and a cane in the other.

Orion returned in early 1853 and resumed control of the paper which was still struggling financially. Orion seldom paid Sam his $3.50 weekly salary because disasters plagued the newspaper. First, a cow broke into the office causing considerable damage, and a subsequent fire ruined the rest of the space. Orion encouraged Sam to write more articles for the paper, but Sam was restless. When a depressed Orion had to move his remaining printing equipment into the living room of the Clemens home, disagreements between the brothers escalated. Their sister Pamela had in 1851 married William Moffett, a wealthy merchant, and moved to St. Louis. Sam decided to join them there and seek a job, although his ultimate goal was to go to New York to see the Crystal Palace Fair.

A view of the 1853 Crystal Palace Fair in New York City *(Library of Congress)*

Eighteen-year-old Sam left home in June 1853. Before he left, his mother made him swear an oath to her on a Bible. She told Sam: "I want you to repeat after me, Sam, these words. 'I do solemnly swear that I will not throw a card or drink a drop of liquor while I am gone.'" Sam agreed because he felt that he was susceptible to both of these vices. In St. Louis Sam got a job on the *Evening News* and began saving money to travel to New York. Two months later he had saved enough for the five-day fare by steamboat and railroad. On August 24, 1853, Sam wrote to his mother telling her that he was in New York and about his experiences getting there. This was the first of many travel letters that Samuel Clemens wrote in his lifetime. Orion published the letter in the *Journal*.

The only job Sam could find in New York was a low-paying one as a journeyman printer in a large printing house. After seeing the sights of New York, he began to spend his evenings at the Printers' Free Library and Reading Room, where he continued his self-education by reading extensively. However, New York did not appeal to him—the long working hours, crowds, and constant noise all bothered him. Less than two months after arriving in New York, Sam moved on to Philadelphia.

Again, he found a job as a printer and wrote long descriptive letters home about the landmarks he saw there. He was not aware that financial problems overwhelmed Orion, who had sold the *Journal*, and moved to Muscatine, Iowa, where he bought a part-interest in the *Muscatine Journal*. He printed Sam's letters in the paper in a column called "Philadelphia Correspondence." Although Sam longed to see his family, he had no money to go home. By summer he could stand his homesickness no longer, left Philadelphia, and visited Orion and his mother in Muscatine. Then he returned to St. Louis and worked a short time for the *Evening News.*

Early in 1855 Sam decided to join Orion one more time in trying to establish a stable family business. The previous December Orion had married Mary "Mollie" Eleann Stotts and had given up newspaper work. He took over the Benjamin Franklin Book and Job Printing Office in Keokuk, Iowa, Mollie's hometown. Their younger brother Henry already worked for Orion, who offered Sam five dollars a week and board to join them. Sam accepted the offer and stayed about a year and a half.

Sam enjoyed his life in Keokuk, making several close friends, but before long he again grew restless. He devoured every book he could find, seeking a place to go for adventure. Finally, he decided he wanted to travel to South America, but he did not have money for the fare. One day as Sam wandered aimlessly down Keokuk's Main Street, a piece of paper blew by and landed on the ground near his feet. When Sam bent to pick up the paper, he discovered it was a fifty-dollar bill. After waiting a few days to see if anyone claimed it, Sam decided it was a sign that he should start his adventure.

Although the unexpected fifty dollars helped with travel, he still needed money for expenses. Recalling that readers had enjoyed his travel letters, Sam decided to seek a newspaper that would pay him to write letters as he headed out for his big adventure. George Rees, editor of the *Keokuk Post*, agreed to pay five dollars for each letter Sam sent. For the next four months Sam sent letters to Rees, using one of his earliest pen names, Thomas Jefferson Snodgrass. Sam depicted Snodgrass as a country bumpkin with terrible spelling and grammar who made mocking comments on big city life.

By the spring of 1857, Sam had saved enough to buy a ticket to New Orleans, where he hoped to board a boat for South America to become a cocoa-hunter on the Amazon River. After purchasing the ticket, Sam had thirty dollars left. He traveled from Cincinnati to New Orleans aboard the steamboat *Paul Jones*, whose pilot was a thirty-one-year-old man named Horace Bixby. Being on the boat revived Sam's childhood dream of becoming a river pilot. From time to time, Bixby allowed Sam to take the wheel. When the trip ended in New Orleans in February, Sam had only ten dollars left. Then he discovered that there was no boat scheduled to go to South America in the near future.

After traveling from Cincinnati to New Orleans on a steamboat, Clemens decided he wanted to become a riverboat pilot. (*Library of Congress*)

Sam searched for Bixby to ask if he could become a cub pilot under the older man's tutelage. At first, Bixby refused the suggestion because having an apprentice was hard work. After several days of Sam's constant persuasion, however, Bixby agreed to teach Sam. The fee was $500, one hundred of which he must pay up front with the remainder to be deducted from his salary when he started earning money. Sam borrowed the one hundred dollars from his well-to-do brother-in-law, William Moffett, and finalized the deal with Bixby.

Sam mastered the river knowledge and on April 9, 1859, earned his pilot's license in less than two years. About nine months prior to that, Sam experienced a tragedy that impacted the rest of his life. He had helped his younger brother Henry get a job as a mud clerk who checked off freight on the steamboat *Pennsylvania*. A few months after he started working, Henry carried a message from the Captain to William Brown, that day's pilot, to make a certain landing. Brown failed to stop at the instructed destination. Since he suffered from deafness, which he refused to acknowledge, Brown did not hear Henry. He denied that Henry had given him the message and struck the boy across the face.

Sam was also on the boat that day, temporarily working as a cub under Brown. Sam was so furious when Brown struck Henry that he grabbed a stool and knocked Brown down. Then Sam started beating the older man with his fists. The boat continued down the river with no one guiding it. Although the Captain agreed that Brown deserved the beating, he could not find another pilot to take over. Unable to leave Sam and Brown together, the Captain asked Sam to get off the boat.

Sam booked passage on the *A. T. Lacey* to get back to St. Louis, but that boat was two days behind the *Pennsylvania* on which Henry still worked. On Sunday, June 13, 1858, witnesses claimed that the *Pennsylvania* was traveling faster than it should when suddenly it exploded. One hundred fifty people died immediately. Henry was among the critically injured. He had originally been thrown out of the wreck into the water, but he tried to swim back to help in the rescue, not realizing how badly burned he was. As Henry approached the boat, scalding steam penetrated his lungs causing them to collapse.

Eventually, Henry was taken to Memphis, where a makeshift hospital had been set up. Sam found him there and "his feelings so much overcame him, at the scalded and emaciated form before him, that he sank to the floor overpowered." Sam sat at Henry's bedside for four days and nights. All the time he sat there, Sam blamed himself for getting Henry the job, for having gotten himself kicked off the *Pennsylvania*, and for not being there to help his brother. Sam telegraphed the news to the family that Henry would not survive. Doctors kept Henry heavily sedated for the pain, and Sam was the one who gave Henry the morphine. When Henry died, Sam again blamed himself, wondering if he had given Henry too much morphine.

Henry's death ended Sam's youth, and his face became so lined that he looked much older than he was. Sam accompanied his brother's body to Hannibal, where Henry was buried beside their father. Despite some of his religious doubts, Sam had remained in the Presbyterian church, even considering going into the ministry at one time. But his brother's death turned his doubts to no belief at all.

THREE
Traveler

After his brother's funeral, Samuel Clemens returned to the river to finish his training. He was never a particularly good riverboat pilot; he ran aground with several boats, and did not seem to have the confidence and aggressiveness of the better pilots. His mentor Horace Bixby commented in later years: "He knew the Mississippi River like a book, but he lacked confidence . . . No sir, Sam Clemens knew the river, but being a coward, he was a failure as a pilot." These harsh words, whether deserved or not, were in direct contrast to Clemens' own recollections: "My life as a pilot on the Mississippi River when I was young—Oh! That was the darling existence. There has been nothing comparable to it in my life since."

Regardless of how capable he was, Clemens' days as a river pilot ended soon after the outbreak of the Civil War. On April

15, Abraham Lincoln called for volunteers for the Union army and established blockades on the Mississippi River. Fearing he might be conscripted by the Union Army to pilot their gunboats, Clemens left the river and went to St. Louis, a city divided in its loyalties. Clemens himself had trouble deciding which side to support, if either. Although his family had a Southern background, Clemens felt loyalty to his nation as well. In mid-June he traveled to Hannibal, where some of his old gang talked him into joining a southern militia they had created that had no ties to the Confederate army.

They named themselves after their county—the Marion Rangers. Unable to organize openly in Hannibal, the fourteen young men went to a neighboring village, New London, to form their battalion. Despite having little equipment or weapons and no leader, they tried to go through the kind of exercises and drills they believed appropriate for a military unit. Success eluded them because they did not know what they were doing. Local farmers supplied them with limited food and a few horses. Always fearful of encountering the enemy, they kept moving and became exhausted from responding to rumors of approaching Union soldiers.

By the second week, Clemens began to doubt the value of their mission. They had accidentally shot and killed a civilian whom they mistakenly believed to be an advance scout for a Union squad. Clemens hurt his ankle when he fell out of a barn where they had spent one night. He had a saddle boil from riding on a horse. Clemens decided to end his enlistment when he realized "that all war must be killing of strangers against whom you feel no personal animosity; strangers whom, in other circumstances, you would help if you found them in trouble." The others agreed with him, and the Marion

Rangers disbanded with no censure because they had never been officially enlisted in the Confederate army. Almost a quarter century later, Clemens described the adventure in "The Private History of a Campaign That Failed."

Still needing a job, Clemens decided to go west with his brother Orion, who had been appointed Territorial Secretary of Nevada as a payback for his political work for Abraham Lincoln.

The brothers arrived in Nevada in August 1861. Because Clemens hoped to make a fortune while he was in the West, he decided to stay in the territory until he became wealthy. For about six months, he actually mined but soon decided that speculating was easier than digging with a pick and shovel. Although he was less than successful, he assured his mother in letters back home that the next strike would be the big one. His mother and sister both urged him to come home and again take up a well-paying position as riverboat pilot. His pride and his confidence that wealth was just around the corner kept him in the West. In a letter to his sister Pamela, Clemens wrote: "I never have *once* thought of returning home to go on the river again, and I never expect to do any more piloting at any price. My livelihood must be made in this country—and if I have to wait longer than I expected, let it be so—I have no fear of failure."

For some time Clemens had sent letters under the pseudonym of "Josh" to the *Virginia City Daily Territorial Enterprise*. When they had an opening, they invited Clemens to come serve as their city editor for a salary of twenty-five dollars a week. Despite his need for money, Clemens did not immediately accept the offer. He was initially afraid to take the job for fear of failing, but he feared not eating more. After thinking about it for over a week, he set out on foot for the 130-mile trek to Virginia City.

When he arrived there on a hot August afternoon, he did not look like much of a journalist. Covered in dust, he wore a slouch hat, a blue wool shirt, and pants hanging over his boots. Exhausted, he dropped into a chair and said: "My starboard leg seems to be unshipped. I'd like about one hundred yards of line; I think I am falling to pieces." As the astonished men looked at him, Clemens continued: "My name is Clemens, and I've come to write for the paper." The memory that he developed as a river pilot now stood him in good stead as he scoured the town for news. Clemens used the myriad of details he remembered to elaborate the smallest of incidents to fill-up space. After about six months, people began to flood into Virginia City following rumors of huge silver lodes. Virginia City became a rough town with rough people, including criminals, and Clemens had no trouble finding material for articles.

However, the Virginia City residents' taste ran more to lampoons, hoaxes, or printed feuds since most of the "news" concerned fights and murders about which the readers already knew. For awhile through a series of letters in print, Clemens carried on a feud with a writer at another newspaper, both using pseudonyms. When the dueling letters became popular, Clemens regretted that readers did not know who was writing them. His editor agreed, and on February 2, 1863, Clemens signed not his real name but "Mark Twain" to one of his letters in the *Enterprise*.

The name came from words that were a nautical expression Clemens had heard frequently as a river pilot. They referred to the depth of the river's water and meant two marks, or twelve feet. The leadsmen chanted the depths as the boat moved slowly: "M-a-r-k three! M-a-r-k three! Quarter-less-three! Half twain! Quarter twain! M-a-r-k twain!" "Mark twain" was the dividing line between safe and dangerous shallow water for steamboats. Although Clemens used the "Mark Twain" pseudonym for almost all of his remaining written work, he sometimes put his real name in parentheses after the pen name, indicating he did not use a different name to hide his identity.

The traits of the writer Mark Twain gradually emerged as he explored various kinds of writing. With the *Enterprise* allowing him to experiment with the fine line between truth and fiction, Twain began to write humorous articles, especially hoaxes. One of them, "The Bloody Massacre Near Carson," fooled his readers who took it as truth. Twain intended it as a satire on mining companies declaring false dividends in order to sell their declining operations. The story he reported as news went like this: *A usually friendly, easy-going man brutally murdered most of his family.* Twain gave the murderer the name of a real man, Mr. P. Hopkins. *When the man's investments began to fail, Mr. P. Hopkins began to change his personality to the point that his wife feared he was going insane. One morning Hopkins rode four miles into town waving his wife's bloody scalp in the air with his throat slit from ear to ear. He could not speak and within five minutes dropped dead in front of a saloon. The sheriff went to Hopkins' house where he found the bodies of Hopkins' wife and seven children.*

The gullible readers believed every word despite the obvious flaws. P. Hopkins was a known bachelor and did not have a wife or children to kill. No one could ride four miles with a slit throat and then survive another five minutes when he got to town. Although hoaxes were common, readers claimed this one went too far. The paper had to print a retraction.

While his editor Joe Goodman was away, Twain got into verbal warfare with James Laird, editor of the *Virginia Union*. After Twain insulted Laird, he waited for Laird to challenge him to a duel. According to the etiquette of that time, an insult required more than a return insult: it demanded a challenge to fight. Twain was not eager to fight, but the *Enterprise* staff finally convinced him to send Laird a challenge. The invitation openly violated a new law that made it a felony to issue or accept a challenge. To make matters worse, when Laird ignored the initial challenge, Twain issued another one. By that time he had convinced himself he wanted to fight.

On the morning the duel was scheduled, Steve Gillis, Twain's friend, took Twain out to practice shooting a pistol at a barn door. As Gillis counted, Twain closed his eyes and fired. He never came close to hitting anything because he would not open his eyes. Then they heard pistol shots and realized Laird was also practicing in the next field. Gillis grabbed Twain's pistol and shot the head off a nearby mud-hen. He handed the pistol back to Twain just as Laird came into view. When Gillis told Laird that Twain had shot the mud-hen at a distance of thirty yards and could do it again, the duel ended. The two men ended up shaking hands and agreeing that others had pushed them into a fight.

However, Twain and Gillis still had to get out of town before the law caught up with them for violating the duel challenge law. Conviction carried a sentence of two years in the penitentiary. The two men left for San Francisco, where Twain believed he could live on some mining stock he still owned. But when the stock crashed, he had to find a job.

Twain became a reporter for the *Morning Call*. He soon discovered that he liked his assignment as the paper's only reporter less than he had liked what he did in Virginia City, where he could at least write a column and features. On the *Morning Call* he divided his day into covering the courts, reporting local news, and reviewing performances at six theaters. He complained that "it was fearful drudgery—soulless drudgery—and almost destitute of interest. It was an awful slavery for a lazy man, and I was born lazy."

While continuing to work for the *Morning Call*, Twain began submitting pieces to other papers, one of which was the *Californian*, a magazine published in newspaper format. Through these submissions, he met Bret Harte, who would become one of America's favorite western writers. Harte later became editor of the magazine and invited Twain to submit articles for twelve dollars a week. But in the meantime, Twain was spending less and less time on his *Morning Call* assignments, and the newspaper fired him in October 1864.

The firing was only the beginning of Twain's troubles. He had no income for two months; the only money he had was a silver ten cent piece that he refused to spend so that he would not have to call himself penniless. He pawned everything he owned except the clothes he wore. Twain avoided his friends because he did not want them to know about his poverty. He refused to ask his family for help because all of his letters to them bragged about how rich he was becoming.

In November his friend Steve Gillis got into a barroom fight in which he badly beat up the bartender. Twain got his friend out of jail on a $500 bond, which he convinced the bondsman he could pay. When the charges changed to assault with intent to kill, Gillis ran away. Knowing he could not cover the bond, Twain left San Francisco also. He hid at the mining camp of Jim Gillis, Steve's brother, located on Jackass Hill, one hundred miles from San Francisco.

Despite being in a mining camp, Twain did not expect riches this time. He realized he had to earn money from his writing. He began to keep a journal of ideas and descriptions, a practice he continued the rest of his life, and submitted stories to various newspapers. At night the men sat around the campfire while Jim Gillis told exaggerated stories as though they were true. Many years later Twain told the stories as part of his own.

In January Twain went with Gillis to Angels Camp in Calaveras County. While Gillis worked a mine he owned

Twain's cabin on Jackass Hill, where he wrote "The Celebrated Jumping Frog of Calaveras County." *(Library of Congress)*

there, Twain sat in the barroom connected to the camp and listened to the miners' stories. A tale that particularly caught his attention was the story of a jumping frog told by an old former riverboat pilot, Ben Coon. Twain recorded the basic details of the story in his journal, never dreaming those few words would bring him fame: "Coleman with his jumping frog—bet a stranger $50.—Stranger had no frog and C. got him one: —In the meantime stranger filled C's frog full of shot and he couldn't jump. The stranger's frog won."

After a few months, Twain decided that he could safely return to San Francisco. Despite having no money, he rejected job offers from morning papers because he did not want to get up early, but he found no openings on evening papers. The *Californian* took a few of his free-lance pieces, but he could not earn enough to support himself. He submitted to various other papers, and as his work appeared more and more, his old paper in Nevada, the *Enterprise*, offered him one hundred dollars a month for letters from San Francisco.

Then he received a letter from humorist Artemus Ward, whom Twain had met in Virginia City when Ward was making a western tour. The two men had much in common, and when Ward started to put together a collection of stories for publication, he remembered Twain and invited him to submit a story. Twain wrote the story about the jumping frog but did not get it to Ward's publishers in time to be included in the book. However, the publisher sent it to his friend Henry Clapp, editor of the *New York Saturday Press*, which published the story on November 18, 1865.

"Jim Smiley and His Jumping Frog" was popular with readers, and other eastern papers reprinted the tale. Then it was

In 1861,Clemens
started working
as the city editor
of the *Virginia City
Daily Territorial
Enterprise*. *(Library of
Congress)*

A view of
Virginia City,
Nevada, in
1866. *(Library of
Congress)*

picked up by the western papers, including the *Californian*, which changed the title to "The Celebrated Jumping Frog of Calaveras County." Soon people across the country began quoting lines like: "I don't see no p'ints about that frog that's any better'n any other frog." Twain himself did not understand all the interest in the story, calling it "a villainous backwoods sketch." He could not see how it was any better than other stories he had written. What he did not realize though was that he had begun to develop one part of his art: the ability to put speech on paper in such a way that the characters came alive. Of course, he did not reject the fame the story brought him from coast to coast.

In San Francisco, a new steamer, the *Ajax*, was getting ready to sail on its maiden voyage to the Sandwich Islands, the original name for Hawaii. The owner invited a select group of people to go on the trip, and with his new fame, Mark Twain was included among them. Twain refused at first but accepted after he convinced the *Sacramento Union* publishers to allow him to be their correspondent on the voyage. He offered to write informative and entertaining travel letters on trade, agriculture, and topics of general interest. They agreed to pay his fare and a small amount for each letter. The publishers also provided him with letters of introduction to important people on the islands.

Knowing he would have a more sophisticated audience in the *Union's* readers, Twain read books about the Sandwich Islands, purchased a language dictionary, and took detailed notes about everything he observed on board the ship. In the midst of his frantic preparation, Twain developed the mumps. The disease slowed him down, but he finished his reading before they docked in Honolulu.

The port of Honolulu, Hawaii, in 1854 *(Library of Congress)*

The beauty of the islands overwhelmed Twain, appealing to his senses as he enjoyed bright fruits and flowers and green trees and grass. The slower pace, compared to that of San Francisco, also appealed to him while he absorbed the "oasis of golden memory" as he called it. Twain sent twenty-five letters back to the *Union*. Most were descriptions or human interest stories. One though was a major scoop of the disaster involving the *Hornet*, a clipper ship that sank in the Pacific Ocean. The *Hornet* caught fire and burned at sea, leaving its thirty-one passengers and crew to crowd into two life boats with only ten days' rations. The fifteen people in the life boat with the ship captain were the only survivors. They reached Honolulu after spending forty-three days on the sea.

When the crew members arrived, Twain himself was in bed with saddle boils suffered while touring on horseback. The United States Minister to China, Anson Burlingame, had Twain carried on a stretcher to the hospital where Burlingame questioned the survivors while Twain took notes. Twain wrote all night to complete the story, and Burlingame just managed to get the manuscript thrown on the deck of the schooner *Milton Badger* as it pulled out of the harbor the next morning headed for California. The *Union* made the scoop a front-page spread across three and a half columns. Twain received $100 per column, ten times his normal rate.

Twain left Honolulu for San Francisco on July 18, 1866. The voyage took twenty-five days, giving him plenty of time to think about what he wanted to do next. Despite the money he had made on the scoop, he did not want to continue in newspaper work. Instead he wanted a job that did not tie him down. He revealed his desire to move on in his journal on the day he arrived in San Francisco: "Home again, No—*not* home again—in prison again—and all the wild sense of freedom gone. The city seems so cramped, & so dreary . . . I wish I were at sea again!"

By the time Twain returned to California, he had gathered more information on the disaster at sea. He used the additional material to write "Forty-Three Days in an Open Boat," published by *Harper's New Monthly Magazine* the following December. Twain had hoped this story would make him known as a "literary" person, not just someone who wrote for a newspaper. Unfortunately, *Harper's* misspelled his name as Mike Swain. Twain had achieved his desire to be a literary person; the problem was that no one knew who he was.

In the next six months, Twain visited with his brother Orion who had come to California to sell Orion's few remaining shares and a house in Carson City, Nevada. Twain gave several lectures about his trip to the Sandwich Islands. For the first lecture in San Francisco, Twain rented the largest theater in the city. When he stepped on the stage, momentary stage fright gripped him as the huge audience applauded wildly. Frozen in place for a moment, Twain realized the noise was friendly and began his lecture. That was Twain's last bout of stage fright.

The lecture that night of October 2, 1866, became the last step in his progress toward becoming one of America's greatest nineteenth-century writers. Into his written works, Twain began to inject the drawling speech that had so charmed the audience. From then on, if his writing seemed dull or trite, he knew how to correct the problem.

Twain left San Francisco in December and headed for New York. He decided to take an around-the-world trip to be financed by writing travel letters. Twain reached an agreement with the *Alta California* that it would sponsor the trip by paying for his transportation and in addition would give him $20 for each of twenty-six letters.

As he boarded the *America,* Twain had no idea that he would soon be traveling on a floating hospital. A cholera outbreak killed thirteen of the six hundred passengers and made hundreds more seriously ill. Fortunately not affected by the disease, Twain spent his time filling his notebooks with conversations, descriptions, observations, and personal notes. The captain, Edgar Wakeman, fascinated Twain, who listened eagerly to Wakeman's assortment of stories. In future works the captain became the model for numerous characters, including Captain Stormfield, and Ned Blakeley in *Roughing It*: "Capt. Ned Blakely . . . sailed ships out of the harbor of San Francisco for many years. He was a stalwart, warm-hearted, eagle-eyed veteran, who had been a sailor nearly fifty years . . . He was a rough, honest creature, full of pluck, and just as full of hard-headed simplicity, too."

Twain arrived in New York in January to find a city vastly changed from the one he had visited thirteen years earlier. He took a quick trip to visit old friends in his boyhood home, Hannibal, before returning to New York to prepare travel letters for the *Alta California* and to look for a publisher of his collected lectures about his trip to the Sandwich Islands. One Sunday he attended a church, where Henry Ward Beecher was the pastor. Beecher, who was a famous Protestant clergyman, appealed to Twain. When he learned that Beecher's church was sponsoring a trip to the Holy Land and Europe, Twain decided to go with them. He asked the *Alta* editors to send him $1,250 for passage. The request surprised the editors, who had agreed to sponsor him on a trip but expected to give him the money in small increments. However, they agreed and Twain applied for one of the one hundred-fifty places on the *Quaker City* which had been reserved for the trip.

At the last minute, two of the main attractions for the voyage, Reverend Beecher and General William Tecumseh Sherman, withdrew from the cruise, causing the tour group to dwindle to seventy-seven people. Twain suddenly became the most famous person on board and was given an upper deck cabin, number ten, originally assigned to the general. The cabin became the center of numerous impromptu gatherings

Henry Ward Beecher *(Library of Congress)*

for the young men on board to smoke, drink, and talk. One of these young men was Charles Langdon, the son of a well-to-do merchant in Elmira, New York. His parents, thinking the cruise was a religious one, had sent Charles, hoping he would mature.

One day Charles showed Twain a picture of his sister Olivia with whom Twain immediately fell in love. He determined to meet the lovely young woman when he returned to the states.

Twain also spent long hours in cabin number ten writing his travel letters. Throughout the trip Twain filled notebooks with details about people and places. He did not stay on the ship all the time and shocked many of his fellow travelers with his irreverent attitude toward places they visited. Twain called the Jordan River a creek and the Dead Sea a fraud. When an Arab boatman wanted eight dollars to provide a ride on the Sea of Galilee, Twain remarked: "Do you wonder now that Christ walked?"

For two of the four months the ship was in the Mediterranean, Twain took tours on land, including a trip through Italy. While he and his companions were ashore in Rome, authorities quarantined the ship in the Bay of Naples because it had traveled to places with cholera epidemics. Twain later described the situation in *Innocents Abroad*, his book based on these travels: "The ship is lying here in the harbor of Naples—quarantined. She has been here several days and will remain several more. We that came by rail from Rome have escaped this misfortune. Of course no one is allowed to go on board the ship or come ashore from her. She is a prison now."

When the ship arrived in Athens, Greece, authorities refused to allow the ship to dock because of the previous quarantine. Twain and a few other passengers used a rowboat to sneak ashore, where they saw the Parthenon and the temples of Minerva and Hercules. From there the ship traveled to Constantinople, Odessa, Yalta, and back to Constantinople to take on more coal. By September the ship had reached Beirut, where Twain and others began the trip to the Holy Land. Here Twain saw his first camel caravan.

The tour group rode by train and donkey to Ephesus, which turned out to be a filthy, disease-ridden place, not the land of milk and honey they had expected. The travelers saw the Jordan River and bathed in the Sea of Galilee. By the time they entered Jerusalem, Twain wrote in his journal: "Thought we never *would* get there." In Jerusalem he saw the Mount of Olives, the Garden of Gethsemane, Calvary, the Via Dolorosa, and bought a small Bible for his mother.

They rejoined the ship in October at Jaffa and sailed for Egypt. After spending five days in Alexandria, they began their return voyage, going first to Gibraltar. Twain and his friends again left the ship to travel through southern Spain and rejoined the ship at Cadiz. The ship did not make any more stops because other ports wanted to quarantine it. The *Quaker City* reached New York City on November 19, the voyage having lasted 164 days.

A nineteenth-century view of Jerusalem, one of the cities Twain visited during his tour of the Holy Land *(Library of Congress)*

As the passengers went their separate ways, they did not realize the disdain for them that Twain had developed over the course of the voyage. He had filled his notebooks with harsh criticism of his fellow travelers' falseness and hypocrisy under the guise of being religious pilgrims. An example of what was to come in his book appeared in a letter Twain sent to the *New York Herald*. He described his traveling companions as pious fakes and their trip as a "funeral excursion without a corpse." The *Herald* printed the letter anonymously, but by then readers easily recognized Twain's style. The book was generally popular though because it provided a moral message in a humorous way in language that people understood.

Upon arriving home, Twain discovered that he had no more royalties due him from *The Celebrated Jumping Frog of Calaveras County and Other Sketches*. He needed an immediate source of income and accepted an offer from Nevada senator William Stewart to come to Washington, D.C., to be the senator's aide while Stewart helped to write the Fifteenth Amendment that gave voting rights to former slaves. As soon as newspapers learned that Twain was in the nation's capital, he received several offers to write letters to the papers. Suddenly, his financial prospects improved.

Twain covered Congress, writing sarcastic descriptions of Washington life that later appeared in *The Gilded Age*:

> Every individual you encounter in the City of Washington almost . . . represents Political Influence. Unless you can get the ear of a Senator, or a Congressman, or a Chief of a Bureau or Department, and persuade him to use his "influence" in your behalf, you cannot get employment of the most trivial nature in Washington. Mere merit, fitness and capability, are useless baggage to you without "influence." . . . It would be an odd

Senator William Stewart *(Library of Congress)*

circumstance to see a girl get employment at three or four dollars a week in one of the great public cribs without any political grandee to back her, but merely because she was worthy, and competent, and a good citizen of a free country that "treats all persons alike."

About the same time that Twain was working in Washington, Elisha Bliss Jr. of the American Publishing Company proposed publishing a subscription book composed of Twain's *Quaker City* letters to the *Alta*. Although the letters had been widely read on the East Coast, few westerners had seen them. While in Washington, Twain contacted Charles Langdon, his fellow traveler on the *Quaker City* excursion whose sister Olivia had so captivated Twain.

Two days after Christmas 1867, Twain accepted an invitation to be a dinner guest at the Elmira, New York, home of Charles's and Olivia's parents, the Jervis Langdons. Meeting Olivia Langdon for the first time only confirmed the strong feelings Twain had experienced upon seeing her picture. Of that initial meeting, Twain later said: "It is

Twain in 1867, around the time *Innocents Abroad* was first published. *(Library of Congress)*

forty years ago. From that day to this she has never been out of my mind."

Twain returned to New York, where he argued with Bliss over contract terms, and worked on gathering, arranging, and editing the *Alta* letters for *Innocents Abroad*. All of a sudden, Twain encountered a problem. The *Alta* publishers did not want to release the letters because they had plans to publish them in a book of their own. Twain made a quick trip to California, where he was able to make arrangements that satisfied everyone.

He faced another problem when he returned to the East Coast. When the directors of the American Publishing Company saw the content of *Innocents Abroad*, they called it blasphemous and wanted Bliss to stop its publication. Bliss stood up to them and threatened to publish the book himself. The directors backed down and with Bliss's able promotion of the book, it eventually became a best seller.

FOUR

Courtship and Marriage

W hile Twain waited for the publication of *Innocents Abroad*, he visited the Langdon family and began to court their daughter Olivia. At first Twain was subtle in his courtship of Olivia, and the elder Langdons did not initially recognize his romantic interest in their daughter. If they had been more aware, the church-going Langdons probably would not have continued to extend invitations to the young man. However, Charles recognized what was happening, and although Twain had been a convivial companion on the *Quaker City*, Charles Langdon did not consider Twain good enough for his sister.

When Olivia was sixteen, she had fallen on ice, injuring her spine. She remained in bed for two years as part of her recovery. Though she was mobile and well when she met Twain, she remained in delicate health. As a result, the entire

Olivia Langdon Clemens
(*Courtesy of AP Images*)

Langdon family was especially protective of Olivia, or Livy as they called her.

Charles, recognizing Twain as a suitor, ordered Twain to leave their home, but a little mishap worked in Twain's favor. As he prepared to depart, he sat down on a carriage seat that was not securely bolted. Twain fell and hit his head on the cobblestone street. Because he was unconscious for a few minutes, the Langdons insisted he remain overnight. Twain agreed because it gave him some extra time to be with Olivia.

Twain later told some friends: "I am desperately in love with the most beautiful girl . . . Unfortunately very rich. She is quite an invalid. I have proposed and been refused a dozen times . . . I know I'm too rough-knocking around the world . . . I never had wish or time to bother with women, and I can give that girl the purest, best love any man can give her. I can make her well and happy." Livy paid little attention to Twain's courtship. However, she determined to spend time turning her brother's friend into a Christian.

Twain knew that he must be solid financially even to dream of marrying Olivia, so he began a lecture tour, earning $100 per night. Between lectures he returned to the Langdon house to see her. When the Langdons realized that their daughter was likely to marry Twain, they started checking into his background. Twain responded to Jervis Langdon's request for references by giving him the names of six people in San

An illustration of Twain on stage during a lecture. *(Library of Congress)*

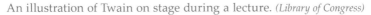

Francisco, two of them ministers. When the responses came back, they were horrible, especially those of the two ministers who criticized Twain's heavy drinking.

Meanwhile Twain continued his lecture tour and his deluge of letters to Livy. He scanned the Bible for quotations, mentioned various hymns, and named churches he had attended. To all appearances Twain was struggling to regain the faith he had lost when his brother Henry died. When Livy's father demanded more references, Twain realized that his California contacts had betrayed him. This time he compiled a list of more outstanding people, including a Supreme Court justice, a governor, and his old *Enterprise* editor Joe Goodman. He assured Jervis: "I think all my references can say I never did anything mean, false or criminal."

Finally, Twain overcame the Langdon's reluctance, and he and Olivia announced their engagement on February 4, 1869. Just a month later, Twain completed his lecture series, having made a profit of $8,000. *Innocents Abroad* appeared in July with sales of 20,000 subscriptions.

Twain next moved to find a strong newspaper connection. When he had the opportunity to purchase a one-third interest in the *Buffalo Express*, his future father-in-law loaned him the $25,000 to do so. Twain served as editor of the *Express* but also made a lecture tour throughout New England. He wanted to pay off all his debts before he and Olivia married.

In Hartford, Connecticut, Twain met a young minister, the Reverend Joseph Twichell, pastor of the Asylum Hill Congregational Church. The two became close friends, a situation that Twain shared in his letters to Livy—he was still working to convince her of his spiritual nature. In fact, during their courtship and early marriage, Twain came as close as

Joseph Twichell *(Courtesy of Yale Collection of American Literature, Beinecke Rare Book and Manuscript Library)*

he ever got to orthodox Christian belief. Livy and Twichell's wife Harmony also became friends.

The couple married on February 2, 1870, with the ceremony taking place in the Langdon home in Elmira, New York, before only a few guests. Reverend Twichell performed the ceremony. Twain and Livy left the next day for Buffalo, where Twain had rented rooms in a boardinghouse, planning to buy a house within the next year. Several other families from the area accompanied the young couple back to Buffalo. These families all lived in prosperous neighborhoods, and Twain could not understand why they were taking Livy and him with them instead of dropping them at the boardinghouse.

As the carriages stopped in front of a beautiful house, Livy's father came out of the house and handed its keys to Twain. As a surprise wedding gift, Jervis Langdon had purchased the fully furnished house for his daughter and son-in-law. He also provided a maid, a housekeeper, a cook, and a

Twain (center) in 1871 *(Library of Congress)*

coachman to be sure his daughter did not have to lower her standard of living. Twain, amazed by Langdon's generosity, told the older man: "Mr. Langdon, whenever you are in Buffalo . . . come right here. Bring your bag and stay overnight if you want to. It sha'n't cost you a cent!"

The couple settled into a pleasant routine. Wanting to keep his bride happy, for the first thirteen months of their marriage Twain observed all the rituals of a religious believer—worship, grace at meals, and Bible reading. Still wanting to prove he could be a financial success and take care of his wife, Twain worked long hours. He wrote various articles for the Buffalo *Express* but also agreed to submit monthly contributions to a magazine called *Galaxy*. For these articles he received an annual payment of $2,400.

News that Mr. Langdon had stomach cancer interrupted the couple's happy life. Livy went to Elmira to help care for her father, who died on August 6. Crushed by the loss of the father she adored, Olivia asked Twain to cancel their summer travel plans. This turned out to be a bad decision because an old friend of Livy's, Emma Nye, came to spend the summer. While she was with the Twains, Emma contracted typhoid fever. Again Livy found herself providing round-the-clock nursing. Despite Livy's loving care, Emma died on September 29. To complicate her life further, the grieving, exhausted Livy discovered she was pregnant.

Another friend came to stay for awhile to cheer Livy up. When the friend finally decided to go home, Livy rode in a carriage with her to the train station. Their carriage was involved in a minor accident, and the doctor put the shaken Livy on bed rest until delivery. The baby, a son named Langdon, was born prematurely and weighed only four and a half pounds at birth. Langdon was in critical condition for several days before he finally began to keep milk down and to gain a few ounces. Afraid little Langdon would not live, Twain waited five days to announce his birth. Twain also worried about Livy, who contracted typhoid fever in addition to recovering from her pregnancy. Despondent, Livy wrote to a friend: "I often feel since Father left us, that he was my back bone, that what energy I had came from him, that he was the moving spring."

Twain needed money to support his growing family, but he knew he could not leave Livy and go on the lecture circuit. He could not write either because he could find no quiet place with the baby constantly crying and various caretakers coming and going. With increased pressure from his publishers to write faster on his next book, *Roughing It*, Twain decided to leave Buffalo. He had never liked the city and now irrationally blamed the town for all his problems. He sold their wedding gift house for just a little more than half its original value and let his partial ownership in the Buffalo *Express* go for $10,000, with $1,000 to be paid immediately and the remainder over the next five years. The Twains went back to Elmira, Livy's hometown, and spent the summer at the Quarry Farm house of her sister Susan Crane.

On the farm Livy grew stronger and became pregnant again. Her first-born, however, grew weaker. Twain had remained in Hartford to finish *Roughing It*, which became the vehicle for the development of the persona of Mark Twain, as distinct from that of Samuel Clemens.

However, that development was a struggle for Twain. On March 4, 1871, he wrote to his brother Orion, who was at that time working for American Publishing Company, Twain's

Quarry Farm house where the Clemenses stayed after selling their home in Buffalo, New York. *(Courtesy of Time & Life Pictures/Getty Images)*

publisher: "Just as soon as ever I can, I will send some of the book M.S. but right in the first chapter I have got to alter the whole style of one of my characters and re-write him clear through to where I am now. It is no fool of a job, I can tell you, but the book will be greatly bettered by it."

The rewrite was to improve the character Mark Twain, who, from the opening page speaks honestly to the reader about his desire for adventure in the West: "I was young and ignorant, and I envied my brother. I coveted his distinction and his financial splendor, but particularly and especially the long, strange journey he was going to make, and the curious new world he was going to explore. He was going to travel!" Thinking he had finally finished the book, Twain discovered that it was approximately five chapters short of the contracted six hundred pages. Twain quickly added notes he had taken on his Sandwich Island tour and sent the book to the publisher. At the same time he received offers to write short pieces and to lecture.

Before he could make a decision, Livy called him to Quarry Farm because little Langdon was critically ill. Somehow the baby survived the crisis, and in the fall of 1871 the Clemenses moved into a house on Forest Street in a Hartford area called Nook Farm. One of their neighbors was Harriet Beecher Stowe, author of *Uncle Tom's Cabin*. Twain's future co-author Charles Dudley Warner and the Reverend Joe Twichell and their families also had homes in the parklike area.

Always looking for a way to make more money, Twain invented a vest strap, which resembled today's suspenders. The elastic strap fastened a man's pants to his vest to keep them from falling down. Twain was so confident about the value of his invention that he went to Washington in early September to apply for the patent in person. Along with most of his other inventions, this one did not bring any financial reward.

In October he began a tour of seventy lectures that, although profitable, were hard on him. Between lectures he became bored and missed his family. At first, he even had trouble choosing lecture topics. Finally, he decided to read excerpts from his recent book, *Roughing It*, a not entirely truthful travelogue of the time he spent in the West. Twain's audiences loved the excerpts as did reviewers.

Charles Dudley Warner wrote in the March 18, 1872, *Hartford Courant*: "*Roughing It* is a volume of nearly 600 pages, of queer stories, funny dialogues, strange, comical,

Charles Dudley Warner *(Library of Congress)*

and dangerous adventures, and it is a book of humor first of all; but we are inclined to think that, on the whole, it contains the best picture of frontier mining life that has ever been written." William Dean Howells echoed a similar opinion in the June 1872 *Atlantic*: "We can fancy the reader of Mr. Clemens's book finding at the end of it . . . that, while he has been merely enjoying himself, as he supposes, he has been . . . acquiring a better idea of the flush times in Nevada, and of the adventurous life generally of the recent West, than he could possibly have gotten elsewhere."

With reviews like these and advanced sales of 20,000 even before the book was published, *Roughing It* seemed set to sell as well or better than *Innocents Abroad*. Although this proved not to be true, Twain finished his lecture tour, determined that from then on, his profession would be author. This decision led him to begin thinking about a book he had wanted to write for a long time—a book about the Mississippi River— its people and events—past, present, and future. Before he could start such an undertaking, though, personal problems confronted him.

First, his brother Orion seemed to uncover fraudulent practices at the publishing house. These practices appeared to cheat Twain out of some royalties. Without talking to his brother, Orion confronted the owner, Elisha Bliss. Although Orion left the company over the issue, whether through dismissal or resignation, Twain chose not to investigate further. He had good sales of his books and feared any legal action against the publisher would kill sales.

While Twain had traveled the lecture circuit, Livy had dealt with the last stages of pregnancy alone. She also worried about Langdon, who seemed developmentally slow. Livy no longer had her faith to comfort her. Although Twain had promised during their courtship that they would lead a Christian life together, the opposite had occurred. Livy's worship had declined, and she seldom attended church. The shared belief that she had sought for their marriage became a shared unbelief, and Twain's commitments made during the first years of their marriage faded.

In March Twain decided to take the family back to Quarry Farm until time for the birth of their next child about six weeks later. However, soon after their arrival in Elmira, Livy went into labor and delivered a daughter, Olivia Susan, on March 19, 1872. Little Susy weighed less than five pounds at birth but quickly doubled her birth weight. Her older brother, sixteen-month-old Langdon, was still sickly. Pale and weak with a chronic cough, he cried constantly. After Susy's baptism near the end of May, the family returned to Hartford.

One day Twain took his young son for a carriage ride, hoping fresh air would be beneficial. Instead Twain did not notice that the baby's blanket had slipped, exposing him to the cold air. Langdon became chilled and developed a chest cold that turned into diphtheria. He died in his mother's arms on June 2. Their friend Joe Twichell held a private ceremony in Elmira, but Livy was too weak to attend. Twain blamed himself for his son's death, repeating the pattern of self-reproach that began when his brother Benjamin died many years earlier.

As the family mourned the loss of their only son, Twain was unable to write. Instead he spent the summer devising the one invention that brought him any money—the Mark Twain Self-Pasting Scrapbook. Tired of assembling scrapbooks with a sticky substance called mucilage, Twain decided to coat the scrapbook pages with strips of dry adhesive that could be dampened without the use of glue. His friend Dan Slote manufactured the scrapbooks that came in more than thirty sizes and models. They first appeared on the market in 1877 with sales of about 25,000, earning Twain approximately $12,000. However, sales declined rapidly after the first year.

With that invention behind him, Twain decided to take a trip to England for two reasons: he might want to write a travel book about that country and he wanted to protect his copyright of *Roughing It* from the English because there was no international copyright law at that time. He went alone

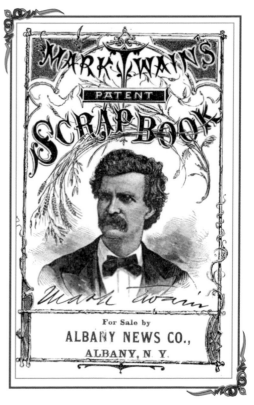

in late August, and the British welcomed him with enthusiasm when he arrived in London. He thoroughly enjoyed the visit which served as a healing time for his grief. Twain never did write a satire about England, perhaps not wanting to offend the people who treated him so well at a low point in his life.

When Twain arrived home in November, he took great interest in the hostile presidential election between incumbent Ulysses S. Grant and contender Horace Greeley, founder of the *New York Tribune* and one of the creators of the Republican Party. Twain had met both men, and although he favored Grant, Twain was a contributor to the *Tribune*. Therefore, he did not get involved in the contest with any written words, although he did in print compliment political cartoonist Thomas Nast, who devised the donkey and the elephant as symbols for the two parties. Greeley died suddenly at the end of the month after losing to Grant.

Despite his lack of direct involvement in the campaign, Twain, like many other Americans, became aware of corruption in the nation's capital. He wanted to write about it but knew he needed a different format from that used in his other two books. Although he had no experience with the genre, he decided to try a novel. Twain sought the assistance of Charles Dudley Warner, a writer and co-editor of the *Hartford Courant*, who had never written a novel either.

The men alternated writing groups of chapters. Twain wrote the first eleven; Warner, the next twelve. By the time *The Gilded Age, A Tale of Today* was completed, Twain had written thirty-two of the book's sixty-three chapters and collaborated with Warner on three others. The theme of the novel concerned possessing Tennessee land—just like the dream Twain's father once had. Squire Hawkins, a key character, speaks words that John Marshall Clemens might have said: "I am leaving you in cruel poverty. I have been—so foolish—so short-sighted. But courage! A better day is—is coming. Never lose sight of the Tennessee Land! Be wary. There is wealth stored up for you there—wealth that is boundless! The children shall hold up their heads with the best in the land, yet." The book also illustrated Twain's genius for satire. He revealed the best and worst of human nature in the postwar corrupt politics of the Grant administration as he showed politicians openly using public trusts for their own private gains.

The problem with two authors writing independently and on such a wealth of topics was that the final work had a mass of unfinished endings. Despite this and other weaknesses, the book, published by Elisha Bliss, had spectacular sales—40,000 copies in the first two months. Twain was not in America, however, to enjoy the book's popularity. He, Livy, and Susy were back in England. While they were gone, architect Edward Potter would build their dream home on property in Nook Farm in Hartford.

While he was in England, Twain planned to arrange for British publication of *The Gilded Age*. However, the process did not proceed as quickly as he had hoped. Despite Livy's wanting to go home, Twain needed to stay in England until a definite publication date was set, or he would lose his copyright. To make the extra time in England worthwhile, Twain gave a series of lectures that lasted until October. At that time Livy insisted they go home because she was two months pregnant.

Twain took her home but immediately turned around and went back to England for another series of lectures. He returned to the United States before the end of the year. However, the new house in Hartford was not ready. They went back to Quarry Farm, where eight-pound Clara was born on June 8, 1874. They were so happy to have a healthy baby but soon realized their joy was premature. Clara could not drink cow's milk, and she became quite ill. Twain and Livy feared losing another child. Livy was trying to gain strength after her pregnancy and caring for a sick child. Suddenly she developed an illness that recurred off and on the rest of the year.

Despite his concern for Livy and Clara, Twain used the summer months productively for writing. His sister-in-law Susan provided him a study—a small, wooden octagon-shaped enclosure somewhat like a pilot house, away from the activities of the farmhouse. In solitude and quiet, he continued work on the first of the three books that immortalized his boyhood on the Mississippi River, a work which would come to be called *Tom Sawyer*.

Throughout the summer of 1874, Twain continued to write, sometimes in bursts of 40,000 words a day, though

The octagonal study at Quarry Farm where Twain would retreat to write. *(Courtesy of Time & Life Pictures/Getty Images)*

without any particular organization. Then without warning in September he hit a writer's block, perhaps because of the lack of an overall plan. He set aside the manuscript, and he and Livy traveled to Fredonia to visit Twain's mother and his sister Pamela. After an exhausting trip, the Twains returned to Hartford to an almost-completed new house. However, workmen were everywhere, and Twain continued to find writing difficult.

When Howells, who edited the *Atlantic Monthly*, the nation's leading literary magazine, asked Twain for a short piece for the first 1875 edition, Twain initially refused. Instead, to get out of the house, he started going for long walks with his friend Reverend Joe Twichell. As they strolled along, Twain told Twichell stories from his river pilot days. The fascinated Twichell remarked: "What a virgin subject to hurl into a magazine!" At that point Twain realized that he could meet Howells' request after all and sent him the first of many such stories.

In return, during the summer of 1875, Twain asked Howells to read the *Tom Sawyer* manuscript. Howells responded:

> I finished reading *Tom Sawyer* a week ago, sitting up till one A.M., to get to the end, simply because it was impossible to leave off. It's altogether the best boy's story I ever read. It will be an immense success. But I think you ought to treat it explicitly *as* a boy's story. . . The adventures are enchanting. I wish *I* had been on that island. The treasure-hunting, the loss in the cave—it's all exciting and splendid.

Twain disagreed though: "It is *not* a boy's book, at all. It will only be read by adults. It is only written for adults."

Livy, who had listened to Twain read every night from the manuscript, agreed with Howells about its being a book for children, and Twain soon concurred. However, he wrote in the novel's Preface: "Although my book is intended mainly for the entertainment of boys and girls, I hope it will not be shunned by men and women on that account, for part of my plan has been to try to pleasantly remind adults of what they once were themselves, and of how they felt and thought and talked."

Samuel Clemens had left behind the scene of his boyhood as soon as he could, but in *The Adventures of Tom Sawyer*,

Inspired by events and people from his childhood, Twain wrote *The Adventures of Tom Sawyer,* which quickly became a popular book with both children and adults. *(Courtesy of Yale Collection of American Literature, Beinecke Rare Book and Manuscript Library)*

Mark Twain looked back upon that childhood with nostalgia. Tom Sawyer was a composite of Sam and his two boyhood friends, Will Bowen and John Briggs. Sam's mother, Jane Clemens, became the prototype for Tom's Aunt Polly, while his father inspired the creation of Judge Thatcher. Uncle Ned, the story-telling slave on the Quarles farm, became Jim in the two novels.

Twain wrote scenes that became known around the world: whitewashing the fence, the cat and the painkiller, the lifting of the schoolmaster's wig, and the discovery of Injun Joe's stolen treasure. Of the episodes in the book, Twain wrote in its preface: "Most of the adventures recorded in this book really occurred; one or two were experiences of my own, the rest those of boys who were schoolmates of mine."

With the publication of *The Adventures of Tom Sawyer* in December 1876, Twain set his stamp upon American literature as a novelist. A reviewer wrote in the *Christian Secretary*: "Those who regard Mark Twain as only a 'funny man' greatly underestimate his power."

FIVE

Author and Investor

Twain's youth increasingly became the subject matter for his books. In addition to *Tom Sawyer* and *The Adventures of Huckleberry Finn*, the first half of *Life on the Mississippi* reflected his days as a cub pilot. He related stories through the eyes of a young person, giving the stories a youthful and innocent perspective.

Although he had begun *The Adventures of Huckleberry Finn* the previous summer, Twain quit working on the novel when he could not decide whether or not he liked the way it was developing. He realized that he needed another approach instead of just a continuation of Tom's adventures told this time by the character of Tom's friend, Huckleberry Finn. Twain did not work on the novel again for several years. He still wanted to write an accurate book about the Mississippi but realized he needed to refresh his memory by returning to the places of his youth from Hannibal to New Orleans.

HUCKLEBERRY FINN.

An illustration of Huckleberry Finn *(Library of Congress)*

Rutherford B. Hayes *(Library of Congress)*

Before making such arrangements, he became interested in the presidential election of 1876, America's centennial year. He became active in the campaign, even marching in a Hartford parade to support Republican nominee Rutherford B. Hayes. Despite rocks thrown at them by supporters of Hayes's opponent, Samuel J. Tilden, Twain said that he had come forward like "nearly all the people who write books and magazines" because he saw "at last a chance to make this government a good government." To Twain's surprise, Hayes

Twain's Hartford home *(Library of Congress)*

did not win the election outright, and the selection went to the House of Representatives which chose Hayes.

Despite his family's final settlement into their Hartford house, Twain was restless. He had trouble meeting the moral expectations of his wife to whom he had given a no-smoking vow before their wedding: "I have to smoke surreptitiously when all are in bed, to save my reputation, & then draw suspicion upon the cat when the family detect an unfamiliar odor." With his book about Huck Finn set aside and any plans for going back to the Mississippi River postponed, Twain tried to achieve some new focus for his writing.

As he waited for inspiration for another book, Twain found himself in serious trouble when his humor got out of hand at a dinner honoring American poet John Greenleaf Whittier on his seventieth birthday. Twain listened as several of America's noted authors rose to praise Whittier and New England literature. Twain found most of the remarks and the ceremony

John Greenleaf Whittier *(Library of Congress)*

boring, so he took his opportunity to speak to tell a humorous story, which he claimed was true. In the tale three other distinguished men at the banquet—Henry Wadsworth Longfellow, Ralph Waldo Emerson, and Oliver Wendell Holmes—were characters, as was Twain. He depicted all four of them arguing, drinking, gambling, and cursing. The men did not find the story funny nor did the rest of the audience, about fifty contributors to the dinner's sponsor, the *Atlantic Monthly*. Twain sensed the growing antagonism of his audience but saw no way out except to finish the story.

Oliver Wendell Holmes *(Library of Congress)*

The next day Twain sent apologies to the three men, all of whom accepted his expression of regret. However, Twain feared he might have ruined any further chances for contributions to the *Atlantic*. This embarrassing episode prompted him to decide it was time to go abroad again. This time he planned to stay a year or two. To save money while in Europe, Twain made arrangements to close down the Hartford house which his family had occupied only a short time. Despite Livy's objections to leaving their new home, the Clemens family sailed from New York in April 1878. Twain rationalized the trip by saying that the cost-of-living was cheaper in Europe and that he needed new materials for another book because *Huck Finn* and *Life on the Mississippi* were at a standstill. Three years had passed since the publication of *Tom Sawyer;* Twain felt he needed a new environment to inspire him.

In 1876, Twain and his family traveled to Heidelberg, Germany, where they stayed for several months. *(Library of Congress)*

Upon arrival in Germany, the family settled in the Schloss Hotel in Heidelberg. All of them attempted to learn the German language, with Twain having more trouble than the others. Although he had rented a room to have a place to write, inspiration did not come. Of the time he spent in Germany, the only part he enjoyed was the five-week walking tour he took with his friend Joe Twichell through the Black Forest into Switzerland. After Twichell went home, the Clemenses moved to Italy for awhile before spending the winter in Munich.

Spring brought a trip to Paris, where the weather remained winterlike, causing them to move on through several other European cities. They came back to London in July and sailed for home on August 23, 1879. Twain took from the trip the beginnings of a new work, eventually titled *A Tramp Abroad*. Even though he had gone to Europe to write a travel book, he had no plan for its organization, and he was not happy with his loose collection of diverse material.

Twain put aside his attempted revisions to the book in order to attend a celebration honoring Ulysses S. Grant. Twain enjoyed all the festivities and then gave a speech to honor Grant that was so good it brought tears and laughter to the audience. Although Twain admired Grant, he did not support his nomination for a third term as president, largely because of the scandals associated with the Grant administration. However, Twain urged him to write his memoirs. In a letter to a friend, Twain concluded: "I couldn't get General Grant to promise to write that book. But he sat down & spun out a lot of secret national history that would make a stunning chapter; says he does want to write that out before it gets too dim in his memory."

After the success at Grant's dinner, Twain had the chance to make up for his former faux pas with America's men of letters. *Atlantic Monthly* decided to honor Dr. Oliver Wendell Holmes at a breakfast. Among the guests were the other two authors whom Twain had ridiculed at the Whittier dinner as well as Whittier himself. This time Twain carefully avoided any but the slightest humor and instead heartily praised Holmes.

Happily settled back in his Hartford home, Twain enjoyed family life, especially games and dramatic productions with his children, and enthusiastically worked on *The Prince and the Pauper*, the story of two young teenage boys in medieval England who look alike and decide to secretly exchange their roles in life. At the same time, Twain struggled to complete *A Tramp Abroad*, his travelogue based on the walking tour he and Joe Twichell took in Europe. In the book Twain used a gentleman narrator who identifies himself only as an American wanting to travel through Europe on foot to study the arts and the German language.

The gentleman views art not through his own eyes but through the eyes of others. In the process Twain managed to attack both European culture and the insincere Americans who excessively flatter it. Twain interrupted the criticism with descriptions of mountain climbs and with stories not related to travel at all, such as the well-known "What Stumped the Blue Jays" about a man who talks to animals. By the end of the narrative, Twain's views of Europe, especially those about manners and food, had become harsher: "Then there is the beefsteak. They have it in Europe, but they don't know how to cook it. . . It comes on the table in a small, round, pewter platter. It lies in the center of this platter, in a bordering bed of grease-soaked potatoes; it is the size, shape, and thickness of a man's hand with the thumb and fingers cut off."

Some of the most humorous passages reflected Twain's own lack of success in mastering the German language. "It's awful undermining to the intellect, German is; you want to take it in small doses, or first you know your brains all run together, and you feel them sloshing around in your head same as so much drawn butter." The title itself carries both ambivalence and humor. "Tramp" could refer to a vagrant wanderer or to a journey on foot. The narrator proposes all sorts of walking trips but always ends up riding in convey-ances ranging from donkey cart to train.

When he completed the manuscript, Twain wrote his friend William Dean Howells, expressing "the unutterable joy of getting that Old Man of the Sea off my back, where he has been roosting for more than a year and a half." At the time of publication, both Europeans and Americans enjoyed *A Tramp Abroad*, which sold more than 62,000 copies in the first year, increasing Twain's transatlantic fame. The sales

Frontispiece illustration of Twain from *A Tramp Abroad*, showing
memories of foreign travel swirling around him as he tries to write.
(Courtesy of Time Life Pictures/Mansell/Time Life Pictures/Getty Images)

reversed a six-year downward trend since the publication of *Innocents Abroad.*

Although it lacked the vivid characterization found in Twain's other books, reviewers on the whole treated it favorably. William Dean Howells indicated an unexpected depth to the book in his *Atlantic Monthly* review: "There is no danger that they [readers] will not laugh enough over it; that is an affair which will take care of itself; but there is a possibility that they may not think enough over it."

In December 1879, still hoping to get rich, Twain invested in a new engraving process called Kaolatype. The procedure involved coating a steel plate with a layer of Kaolin, or china clay. After cutting an image in the metal, the operator poured melted metal into it. The cold metal then formed a die for printing engravings like the ones used in Twain's books. Believing the invention would revolutionize the engraving process, Twain formed the Kaolatype Engraving Company with himself as the president and chief stockholder. Although the chalk plate process was a brilliant idea, other better, less-expensive photographic etching techniques soon bypassed it. By the time Twain realized the company was a failure, he had lost $50,000.

The Clemens family always spent summers in Elmira. It was there on July 26, 1880, their third daughter was born— Livy almost died during the delivery. They named the child Jane Lampton Clemens after Twain's mother, though the family always called her Jean. During that summer Twain alternated working on two books, *The Adventures of Huckleberry Finn*, which he had set aside years earlier, and *The Prince and the Pauper.* Considering the latter book the better of the two, Twain read to his family from it each night.

Twain's three daughters *(Yale Collection of American Literature, Beinecke Rare Book and Manuscript Library)*

A notebook entry on November 23, 1877, first revealed Twain's idea for such a story: "Edward VI and a little pauper exchange places by accident a day or so before Henry VIII's death. The Prince wanders in rags and hardships and the pauper suffers the (to him) horrible miseries of princedom, up to the moment of crowning in Westminster Abbey, where proof is brought and the mistake rectified." The two main characters, Tom Canty, a beggar from Offal Court, and Edward VI, son of Henry VIII and heir to the throne, resemble each other so much that when they exchange clothes, even their parents do not recognize the difference. Set in England in the early part of the sixteenth century, *The Prince and the Pauper* is the only one of Twain's books that is not at least partially autobiographical. Twain dedicated the book to his daughters, Susy and Clara, who listened to him read every word aloud.

In October Livy hired as a maid Katy Leary, who had previously served in the home of Livy's brother, Charles Langdon. Katy would stay with the Clemens family for the next thirty years as nursemaid, seamstress, and nanny. About that same time, Twain traveled to Washington, D.C., to seek assistance for an international copyright law. An old friend, Representative Rollen Daggett, agreed to back such a bill if Twain could get authors to agree on what they wanted. Twain found that he could not make up his own mind on certain issues so dropped that pursuit to become involved in the 1880 presidential election in support of James A. Garfield.

After spending some time campaigning for Garfield, and giving an inspiring speech in Hartford, Connecticut, Twain returned to focusing on his own financial affairs. He decided to sever his ties with the American Publishing Company, claiming that they were not working hard enough to sell his books. Instead he let James R. Osgood publish *The Prince and the Pauper.* Although Osgood had an impressive list of authors that he published, he was not a good businessman. Twain ended up advancing money to pay the publication costs and paying Osgood a royalty for selling the book.

The Prince and the Pauper was published in England in 1881 prior to its 1882 issue in the United States. Despite his departure from his usual humorous style, Twain received favorable reviews for the most part. The *Hartford Courant* reported: "Mark Twain has finally fulfilled the earnest hope of many of his best friends, in writing a book which has other and higher merits than can possibly belong to the most artistic expression of mere humor." The *New York Herald* agreed: "To those who have followed the career of Mark Twain, his appearance as the author of a charming and noble romance is really no more of a surprise than to see a stately structure risen upon sightly ground . . . The character of these two boys, twins in spirit, will rank with the purest and loveliest creations of child-life in the realm of fiction."

Only his old friend and mentor, Joe Goodman, editor of the *Virginia City Enterprise*, disagreed openly, saying that he was disappointed and hoped that Twain would come to his senses and get back to what he ought to be writing about. Twain himself considered the book his best up to that time and had enjoyed writing it so much that he had been in no hurry to finish it. In her book about her father, young Susy wrote: "it is unquestionably the best book he has ever written."

Always seeking wealth, Twain invested in several more inventions—a patent steam generator, a steam pulley, and a watch company. All failed, and he lost money. He chose not to invest with a young inventor, Alexander Graham Bell, who was seeking investors for his telephone; instead, Twain began to invest in the Paige compositor that set type automatically. Over the next decade he poured a great deal of his income into the machine, though it never caught on and gave Twain a return on his investment.

Twain decided to return to the Mississippi to renew his acquaintance with the mighty river. After reaching New Orleans, which was still the same dirty, crowded place he remembered, Twain found Horace Bixby, the man who had taught him to be a riverboat pilot. Twain arranged to travel upriver with Bixby. On the trip he filled his notebooks with detailed information before taking quick side trips to Hannibal and Keokuk, where his brother Orion lived with his family. The changes in Hannibal, his boyhood home, brought tears to his eyes. Young boys no longer dreamed of becoming river boat pilots as he and his friends had done. Instead the youth wanted to be railroad engineers. One thing about Hannibal had not changed though—the same old mud still covered the streets.

Twain returned to Hartford, where he expected to write the river book quickly. However, several interruptions slowed the process. First, daughter Jean caught scarlet fever; soon the disease spread to other household members, and Twain had to help Livy with nursing care. Then Twain himself started feeling ill and had to struggle to write the 30,000 additional words he needed.

Even though he had not completed the work about the Mississippi River, he decided to start sending finished chapters to a typist. This manuscript was among the earliest typed literary manuscripts by any author. In January 1883 the typist returned the last pages for proofing, and the book was published in May. Although initial sales were not good, over the years *Life on the Mississippi* sold many copies.

At first glance *Life on the Mississippi* appears to be a variety of basically true and factual incidents told by a first person narrator. Although the events represent the narrator's experiences, he merely relates them and does not seek any sort of self-analysis. The first twenty chapters reflect Mark Twain's early experiences as a cub pilot and later as a pilot on the Mississippi River. The process of learning, growing, and developing as a pilot changes the narrator's impression of the river:

> Now when I had mastered the language of this water, and had come to know every trifling feature that bordered the great river as familiarly as I knew the letters of the alphabet, I had made a valuable acquisition. But I had lost something, too. I had lost something which could never be restored to me while I lived. All the grace, the beauty, the poetry, had gone out of the majestic river!

The narrator illustrates this realization with before and after descriptions. A beautiful sunset had once turned a "broad expanse of the river . . . to blood;" then with knowledge he sees the sun as meaning only "that we are going to have wind to-morrow."

In chapter twenty-two, Twain takes the reader forward twenty-one years to his visit to the Mississippi River after that long an absence. Amongst comments about changes on the river, Twain describes a house through the eyes of Charles Dickens, assaults southern chauvinism, blames Sir Walter Scott for the Civil War, talks about Joel Chandler Harris's Uncle Remus stories, describes incidents from his childhood, and tells myths and tall tales.

Twain had initially struggled to get the required 80,000 words for the book. By the time it was finished, perhaps because of its loose organization, he found the manuscript to be too long and told his publisher Osgood to cut whatever he wanted. Osgood and his editors deleted 15,000 words. Later, Twain tried to rewrite parts of the book, but that undertaking was never completed.

Reviewers, for the most part, were favorable. The *Chicago Tribune* stated that *Life on the Mississippi* "imparts a great deal of useful information, and . . . is much more than a mere

Twain with Livy and their daughters in 1884 *(Courtesy of Yale Collection of American Literature, Beinecke Rare Book and Manuscript Library)*

'funny' book." Longtime friend and critic William Dean Howells dug a little deeper for the significance of what Twain had done in this book: "So far as I know, Mr. Clemens is the first writer to use in extended writing the fashion we all use in thinking, and to set down the thing that comes into his mind without fear or favor of the thing that went before or the thing that may be about to follow."

Many years later, when Twain's obituary appeared in the *Glasgow Herald* in Scotland, a reporter said: "I shall certainly reread many times the altogether delightful *Life on the Mississippi*, which as regards sheer writing takes rank with some of the finest prose . . . and remains the best of the class to which it belongs."

With *Life on the Mississippi* completed, Twain was newly enthusiastic about his work and energized by his revived memories of the Mississippi River. Twain started to work once again on *The Adventures of Huckleberry Finn*, which he had set aside seven years earlier. Suddenly the words came faster than he could write, and he believed he could finish the novel in two months. He told his friend Howells: "*I* shall like it, whether anybody else does or not."

Set in the mid-nineteenth century, before the Civil War, the novel is the story of a young, white, uneducated boy, Huck Finn, who helps Jim, a slave, to escape being sold. In the course of the novel, Twain explores such topics as slavery, race relations, moral principles, greed, and corruption. Though humorous, like much of Twain's other work, the novel took on much deeper themes than Twain had explored previously—indeed, many argue that the novel really is about the search for freedom.

The story begins in St. Petersburg, first with a continuation of the action of *The Adventures of Tom Sawyer* followed by Huck's escaping his father's brutality. It ends about a year later after Huck and Jim have traveled on a raft over a thousand miles down the Mississippi River, occasionally stopping to go ashore for adventures on land. The narrative is mostly episodic, jumping from one scenario to the next without a major overriding plot to hang it together, other than the frame of Huck and Jim traveling down the Mississippi. Twain famously addressed the book's untraditional structure in a notice on the first page, writing "Persons attempting to find a motive in this narrative will be prosecuted; persons attempting to find a moral in it will be banished; persons attempting to find a plot in it will be shot."

For its narration, Twain wrote from Huck's perspective, making use of many regional dialects to realistically portray the characters and the way they speak. This is apparent throughout the text, such as this section in Chapter Six in which Huck discusses his father and the possibility of living with the widow Douglas:

> Pap warn't in good—so he was his natural self. He said he was down to town, and everything was going wrong. His lawyer said he reckoned he would win his lawsuit and get the money, if they ever got started on the trial; but there was ways to put it off a long time, and Judge Thatcher knowed how to do it. And he said people allowed there'd be another trial to get me away from and give me to the widow for my guardian, and they guessed it would win, this time. This shook me up considerable, because I didn't want to go back to the widow's any more and be so cramped up and sivilized, as they called. Then the old man got to cussing . . .

Published in 1885, the reviews for *Huckleberry Finn* were generally good—the *Hartford Courant* claimed "Mr. Clemens has made a very distinct literary advance over *Tom Sawyer*, as an interpreter of human nature and a contributor to our stock of original pictures of American life." Many other critics of Twain's day praised it as his best work yet, though some were put off by the use of dialects, and found some of the episodes in the book too dark.

Regardless of reviews, *The Adventures of Huckleberry Finn* proved to be Twain's most controversial work. Shortly after the novel's publication, several libraries and communities, most notably the Library Committee of Concord, Massachusetts, banned the book. They claimed to find it "rough, coarse and inelegant, dealing with a series of experiences not elevating, the whole book being more suited to the slums than to intelligent, respectable people." Author Louisa May Alcott agreed with the decision, declaring: "If Mr. Clemens cannot think of something better to tell our pure-minded lads and lasses, he had best stop writing for them."

Twain was unperturbed by the controversy, believing that the banning would only cause more people to want to read *Huck Finn*. Sales figures seemed to prove him right—51,000 copies were sold in the first few months. As the *Hartford Courant* pointed out, "The public library committee of Concord, Mass., have given Mark Twain's new book, *Huckleberry Finn*, a wide advertisement by refusing to allow it to be put on their shelves. The result will be that people in Concord will buy the book instead of drawing it from the library, and those who do will smile not only at the book but at the idea that it is not for respectable people."

Despite its success, the novel continued to be controversial, and is frequently challenged or banned even today. This is largely due to the book's frequent usage of the racial epithet "nigger," and what is seen as the novel's racist perspective. Evidence in the text suggests that Twain was not racist, though. For one, with his use of dialect and realistic dialogue, he sought to accurately represent the speech and vocabulary of people in the pre-Civil War Mississippi River area, and doing that required using not only a derogatory racial term, but other words also considered vulgar.

Furthermore, Twain hoped to comment on the racism he saw in his own time: in the post-Civil War era in which

Twain wrote, equal rights continued to evade black people. They were routinely lynched by racist whites, and imprisoned blacks were leased as laborers in the South, re-creating the slavery that the war was supposed to have ended. With *Huckleberry Finn* and the character of the slave Jim, though, Twain created a vivid portrait of a black man forging a friendship with a white boy. Many critics point out that the usage of the offensive word may be intentional to show how the society denies Jim of his humanity, but by the novel's end, though Huck continues to use the derogatory word to describe Jim, he has come to recognize Jim as a fellow human being with dignity, who deserves freedom and happiness—Huck is even willing to risk his own safety to help Jim get his freedom. Furthermore, Jim is one of the book's most honorable and decent characters, standing in stark contrast to the various murderers and con-men that Huck and Jim encounter on their journey.

With time, *Huckleberry Finn* has become Twain's most acclaimed book. Regarded by many reviewers as one of the best and most important novels in American literature, it had sold 20 million copies by the 1990s, a number that continues to grow as the book continues to be a staple of high school and college reading lists. Nobel Prize-winning author Ernest Hemingway said: "It's the best book we've had. All American writing comes from that. There was nothing before. There has been nothing as good since."

SIX

Financial Struggles

A year before *Huckleberry Finn*'s publication, Twain grew fed up with what he perceived as a lack of effort from his publisher James Osgood in selling his books, and decided to start his own publishing company. Twain didn't want to run it himself, though, so in May 1884, he installed his nephew by marriage, Charles Webster, as the head of the new firm, to be called Charles L. Webster and Company. *The Adventures of Huckleberry Finn* was the first book published by the new firm.

Webster and Company quickly became established as one of America's main presses with the publication of Ulysses S. Grant's autobiography. Twain had initially approached Grant about writing his memoirs some years earlier, but Grant had declined. Two episodes in Grant's life—a failed business and the development of throat cancer—caused him to change his mind. Grant feared that should he die, he would

Ulysses S. Grant's autobiography, published by Twain's publishing company, became a huge success, and its profits allowed Twain to pay off his debts. *(Library of Congress)*

not have enough money to provide for his family. Grant had a contract with another publisher, but Twain convinced him that the other company had underestimated the volume of sales Grant's memoirs would bring. Grant finally agreed to let Charles L. Webster and Company publish his book, and Webster gave him an advance payment of $1,000. Only much later did Twain learn that the money had provided food for Grant's almost penniless family.

To escape creditors taking his book's royalties, Grant transferred ownership of them to his wife. Then Grant pushed himself to complete the two-volume work before his death. Not long after completing the work, Grant died on July 23, 1885, and there was an immediate interest in the work: Webster and Company worked night and day to meet the demand, and some 320,000 copies of *Personal Memoirs of Ulysses S. Grant* were sold. Grant's widow received an initial payment of $200,000, the largest single royalty check ever paid up to that time. Three months later, she received a similar check, bringing the total royalties to $400,000. After covering all the production costs, Twain made about $100,000 and was finally able to pay off his debts.

With his financial situation improved, Twain became a partner in a company to manufacture and distribute the Paige typesetter, in which he had earlier invested. Optimistic projections about possible sales of the machine filled his notebooks. In his dreams the profits were always in the millions. Twain encouraged his friends to invest also. His commitment to the machine showed his faith in its future, but he ignored the fact

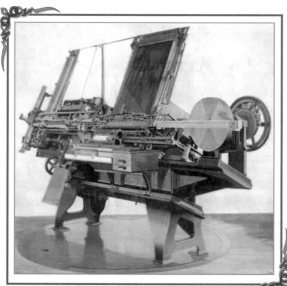

Twain poured money into the development of the Paige Typesetter, but the machine was never sucessful.

that other inventors were working on similar and perhaps simpler machines. Twain began several years of heavy monetary investment in what eventually proved to be a failure.

After the success of Grant's autobiography, Twain decided a similar book of memoirs written by the Pope would be even more profitable because every Catholic would probably want a copy. Twain sent Webster to Rome to negotiate for Pope Leo XIII's authorized biography. The plan was to publish the book in six languages with each book being blessed by the

Pope Leo XIII *(Library of Congress)*

Pope. Without having researched the market, Twain's company signed a contract in spring 1886. The actual sales barely covered the expenses of publication, and the company needed another Twain book to compensate for lack of sales. But Twain had been so busy with publishing other people's books and buying into the Paige typesetter he had not been writing. In her biography of her father, Susy wrote: "Mamma and I have both been very much troubled of late because papa, since he has been publishing Gen. Grant's book, has seemed to forget his own books and work entirely."

Knowing that the lecture circuit brought in sure money, Twain went on a reading tour with G. W. Cable, an author noted at the time for his portrayal of Louisiana Creoles. While they were together, Cable introduced Twain to a book about medieval England, Sir Thomas Malory's *Le Morte D'Arthur*. Twain had already recorded in his notebook an idea for a medieval England story:

> Dream of being a knight errant in armor in the Middle Ages. Have the notions and habits of thought of the present day mixed with the necessities of that. No pockets in the armor. Can't scratch. Cold in the head—can't blow—can't get a handkerchief, can't use iron sleeve. Iron gets redhot in the sun—leaks in the rain, gets white with frost and freezes me solid in winter. Makes disagreeable clatter when I enter church. Can't dress or undress myself. Always getting struck by lightning. Fall down and can't get up.

Malory's book convinced Twain to develop his idea further, and he began to work on a book set in the Medieval era. Although he had planned to write it quickly, he did not complete *A Connecticut Yankee in King Arthur's Court* for several

Hoping to bring in some money after the failure of Pope Leo XIII's autobiography, Twain went on a lecture tour with G. W. Cable (right). *(Yale Collection of American Literature, Beinecke Rare Book and Manuscript Library)*

years. After making an initial effort on the book, Twain set it aside when he learned his mother was seriously ill. He took his daughters to Keokuk to visit their grandmother, whom they did not often see.

After reading about Queen Victoria's Jubilee in 1887, Twain was reminded of all the things he did not like about

An illustration from *A Connecticut Yankee in King Arthur's Court* (*Library of Congress*)

England's ruling class (first fostered by his travels abroad as a young man). These strong emotions sent him back to working on *A Connecticut Yankee*, which criticized not only nineteenth-century oppression but medieval superstition as well. With renewed enthusiasm, he turned out twenty chapters by mid-summer. During this period, he accepted a master of arts degree from Yale University in recognition not only of his writing but of his sponsorship of a young African American youth through Yale law school. After the ceremony, he returned to his fast-paced writing, hoping to finish *A Connecticut Yankee in King Arthur's Court* by October.

Twain's financial situation, however, prevented the book's completion at that time. Webster and Company had not produced a best seller since Grant's memoirs. Twain had been putting his own money into the operation to keep it afloat, although he had never intended to use his royalties to support the company. He began to blame Charles Webster for poor management. In early 1888 he made Webster take a leave-of-absence for health reasons and replaced him with Frederick Hall. By the end of the year, Webster was no longer associated with the publishing firm that bore his name.

Meanwhile, Twain continued to give more money to the Paige Typesetter's inventor, James W. Paige, who promised completion on the machine by April 1888. The invention should have been ready, but Paige was a perfectionist who kept delaying use of the machine to make minor adjustments. By that time Twain had invested more than $80,000 in the machine, ignoring the fact that the *Chicago Tribune* had already ordered twenty-three linotype machines to do the same job that the Paige was intended to do. With Twain's money going toward the typesetter, he and Livy dipped heavily into her investments to pay their Hartford house expenses of $35,000 a year and to keep the publishing company going. Despite his family's being affected by all the money going to the typesetter, Twain did not give up. The typesetter became for him what the Tennessee land had been for his father: the promise of wealth and security for his family.

In January 1889, the machine finally appeared ready, and Twain attended a demonstration that caused him to write glowing letters to his family and friends. Then the machine started breaking the type. Paige said the problem was only a minor glitch but that he would have to take the machine apart to fix the problem. This meant rehiring the crew of men who had been working on the machine at a cost of more than $3,000 per month. Twain continued to support him.

In March, the twenty-five-year-old daughter of Twain's friend William Dean Howells died, and in July Twain's brother-in-law Theodore Crane died. The two deaths so close together caused Twain to reconsider his beliefs about God, and in a letter to Livy he came as close to an affirmation of belief as he had since their courtship. "Dear, dear sweetheart, I have been thinking & examining, & searching & analyzing, for many days, & am vexed to find that I more believe in the immortality of the soul than misbelieve in it." Some question the sincerity of his statement though: he wrote in his notebook at about the same time: ". . . myriads have believed in it [immortality]. They also believed the world was flat."

Near the end of 1889, Twain finished *A Connecticut Yankee in King Arthur's Court.* It is a framed story: a narrator introduces the reader to a story within a story. Action begins when Hank Morgan, a foreman in a Colt pistol factory, gets hit over the head with a crowbar by a man named Hercules. The blow transports Morgan from 1879 Connecticut to sixth-century England. Because of his nineteenth-century skills and knowledge, Morgan becomes the King's aide, known as The Boss. Morgan cannot resist showing off innovations of his own time, such as a daily paper, dynamite, and bicycles.

The story begins as a satire poking fun at the customs and institutions of feudal England. As Twain tries to implant modern American technology and political ideas into sixth-century England, he savagely attacks all institutions and viewpoints that support a monarchy, privileged classes, bondage of any kind, and established churches. Although he holds up democracy as the preferred way of governing, Twain does not picture it as perfect, contending that laws still benefit the few rather than the many. Because the book reflects a variety of Twain's political and social ideas developed over a span of years, it is his most complex effort as well as his most fragmented. As usual, his friend, critic Howells, praised the effort: "It's charming, original, wonderful—good in fancy, and sound to the core in morals."

British critics did not agree. Twain's mocking imitation of the Round Table offended many, and his English publishers begged Twain to revise the book for publication in England to remove those parts most offensive to the British. Twain refused, feeling he had spent enough time on the book already. However, even he was not completely satisfied, although for different reasons. Just before publication, he wrote to Howells: "Well, my book is written—let it go. But if it were only to write over again there wouldn't be so many things left out. They burn in me; and they keep multiplying & multiplying; but now they can't ever be said."

After the book's publication, another comic writer, Charles Heber Clark, who wrote under the pseudonym Max Adeler, accused Twain of plagiarizing *The Fortunate Island*, a novella Clark had written almost ten years earlier. Twain denied any knowledge of the other man's work.

Having written *A Connecticut Yankee* at a furious pace, Twain developed rheumatism in his shoulder and arm, making further writing difficult. The entire family went with him to the Catskill Mountains for the summer to allow Twain to relax. A call to come to his mother's bedside interrupted their vacation. Twain went to Keokuk, where his mother, Jane

Clemens, died on October 27, 1890, after years of suffering and illness. More bad news followed. Livy's eighty-seven-year-old mother died a month later in Elmira, and daughter Jean suffered the first of many epileptic seizures.

By this time Twain was having trouble raising funds to support Paige's constant repairs and changes on the typesetter. Up to this point Twain had invested more than $190,000 for nothing. For the first time in twenty years, Twain was totally dependent on his writing for income. As financial worries consumed his thoughts, his rheumatism pain worsened. In the meantime he poured money into the typesetter while the publishing company failed to realize a profit. In December Twain wrote to Fred Hall, his publishing house manager: "Merry Christmas to you, and I wish to God I could have one before I die."

Twain encouraged Hall to move forward with getting a patent both in the United States and abroad for a history game that Twain invented. It had started as an outdoor game to teach English royal genealogy and the length of each king's reign to his children. Wooden pegs marked a king's tenure so that they could easily determine the length of each king's rule by observing the distance between the pegs. Twain's children loved playing the game on the slopes of Quarry Farm. Then Twain tried to convert it to a board game that he believed would bring him millions of dollars in royalties.

He wanted to produce many games about the lives of famous people, such as kings of other nations, statesmen, churchmen, and celebrities. Each game would contain one thousand facts and would have an accompanying book with 8,000 facts. He envisioned people organizing clubs to compete with one another in the games. However, his plans were too grandiose, and he was unable to make his ideas into a playable board game. In later years, remarking on the failure to realize his dream about the game, he said: "I might have known it wouldn't be an easy job, or somebody would have invented a decent historical game long ago—a thing which nobody *had* done."

In early 1891, Twain decided that he could reduce expenses by taking his family to live in Europe for awhile. His wife and three daughters were not happy about the move. Clara later wrote: "We all regarded this break in a hitherto harmonious existence as something resembling a tragedy." Nevertheless, Twain shut down the Hartford house completely, dismissing all the staff except a caretaker and Katy Leary.

As they sailed from New York in June, Twain realized that the purpose of this voyage was different from that of previous ones. This time he had to get his finances in order and learn not to repeat past mistakes. Writing another book was one way he could make money, but he continued to suffer from his rheumatism, making holding a pen almost impossible. To gain some immediate cash, he had contracted with William Laffan at the *New York Sun* to write six articles on various topics with each submission bringing him $1,000.

After settling in Paris, Twain and Livy visited a health spa, hoping that Twain would get rid of his pain and that fragile Livy would grow stronger. The family went to Berlin in October. They chose the German town because of its reputation for good music and good doctors. Daughter Clara had shown some musical talent and became the student of a well-known pianist. Susy, who had left behind her friends at Bryn Mawr when the family moved, was depressed much of the time. She especially missed her best friend, Louise Brownell. Jean studied with a tutor.

During his time in Europe, Twain became deeply interested in the story of Joan of Arc, and decided he wanted to write a book about her. He poured himself into learning about her and the time in which she lived, doing more research than he had for any subject previously. He wrote some 100,000 words, in six weeks, almost completing the first part of what would become a three-part book. But then he had to set the book aside, as he was planning a trip to America.

He traveled to New York the following spring to see what he could do about the publishing house's continued loss of money. He also went to Chicago, where the typesetter was supposedly ready. Paige reported to Twain that he had found new backers to form a company to manufacture the typesetter. Twain had planned to get rid of his royalties in the machine but decided to investigate Paige's claim further. He learned that a factory had been started and planned to manufacture fifty typesetters. Twain did not have time to do a thorough investigation of the company because he became ill with a bad cold and spent most of his time in the hotel room. Paige visited Twain and convinced him that millions of dollars were in their future. After Paige's visit, Twain wrote in his notebook: "What a talker he [Paige] is! He could persuade a fish to come out and take a walk with him. When he is present I always believe him— I cannot help it." Twain decided to hold on to his shares for a while longer.

Upon his return to Europe, Twain began work on a story that became *Tom Sawyer Abroad*. When he received an offer from the well-regarded children's magazine *St. Nicholas* to let them serialize the story, he accepted. However, before he

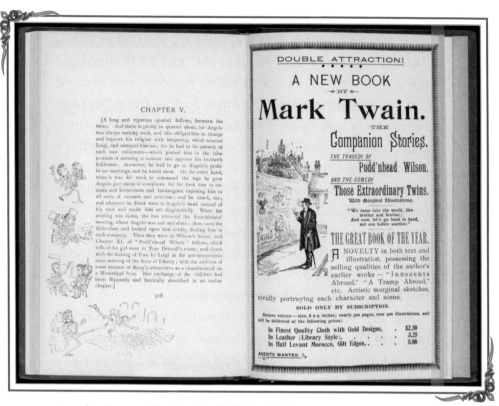

An advertisement for Twain's *Pudd'nhead Wilson* *(Yale Collection of American Literature, Beinecke Rare Book and Manuscript Library)*

finished that story, he started on another book. Originally called *Those Extraordinary Twins* when first written in 1869, the story followed the comic problems of conjoined twins. However, as Twain developed the story, other minor characters began to assume more importance, and the twins became almost insignificant. The new version was the beginning of *Pudd'nhead Wilson.*

By 1893 the United States was in the grip of a terrible depression, causing the publishing business to deteriorate further. Twain made numerous trips between Europe and the

United States, trying to save his investment. But the company was $200,000 in debt and had only $50,000 in assets. Twain offered to let Hall buy him out, but Hall declined and put pressure on Twain not to sell to someone else because that would endanger Hall's position. Just as Twain began to believe there was no hope, he met Henry Huttleston Rogers, vice-president of Standard Oil Company and one of America's wealthiest men.

Rogers was a Twain fan, and the two men immediately liked each other. Twain reflected on their first meeting: "We were strangers when we met, and friends when we parted, half an hour afterward." Twain came away from that initial meeting not only with a new friend but with a check for $4,000 so that he could pay his most pressing debts.

Because of his problems, Twain had not given full concentration to *Pudd'nhead Wilson*, the book he believed could pull him out of his financial quagmire. He wrote at a frantic pace, and the story changed drastically from his initial conception of it as he wrote. He dropped the conjoined twins and substituted two formerly minor characters. One of them became the principal character after whom Twain named the book.

Like *Tom Sawyer* and *Huck Finn*, the novel was set in a small Missouri town, Dawson's Landing, before the Civil War. It sarcastically and ironically dealt with such subjects as small-town prejudice, slavery, lost birthrights, and distorted parental love. Twain developed one of the main topics, the effect of learning on a person's development, by having two babies switched in infancy.

Similar to *The Prince and the Pauper*, *Pudd'nhead Wilson* concerns the swapping of two unrelated boys—one from a privileged background and the other the child of a slave.

Henry H. Rogers, circa 1890 *(Courtesy of Getty Images)*

However, the slave mother's gift to her child of a white identity ends in destruction. In addition to the story of the switched boys, the novel has two other separate story lines: the arrival in Dawson's Landing of a young lawyer who makes a fool of himself in front of the villagers, resulting in his alienation and their designating him "pudd'nhead," and the arrival of Italian twins (all that remained of the original twin idea). Twain develops each of the three stories individually, but they intersect from time to time. The multiple plots each deal with the theme of the confusion of moral identity. When he decided on the idea of switching the rich and slave babies, Twain developed a racial motif that he had not earlier intended and knew he would have to rewrite the first part of the book to match the last segment. He told a friend: "I've finished that book & revised it. The book didn't cost me any fatigue, but revising it nearly killed me."

In August 1893, he wrote to his manager: "I mean to ship 'Pudd'nhead Wilson' to you—say tomorrow. It'll furnish me hash for a while I reckon. I am almost sorry it is finished; it was good entertainment to work at it, and kept my mind away from things." In December, *Century* magazine began serial publication of *Puddn'head Wilson*, for which they paid Twain $6,500.

During the following year, Twain's new friend Henry Rogers looked into the situation with the Paige typesetter. At first he thought there might still be possibilities for the machine and sent a telegram to Twain with that news. Upon hearing the report, Twain wrote to Livy: "I and mine, who were paupers an hour ago, are rich now & our troubles are over!" However, before committing further on the machine, Rogers wanted to see it tested at the

Chicago Herald, where thirty-two linotype machines were already working.

After his visit, Rogers said:

> Certainly it [the typesetter] was a marvelous invention. It was the nearest approach to a human being in the wonderful things it could do of any machine I have ever known. But that was just the trouble; it was too much of a human being and not enough of a machine . . . It was too costly; too difficult of construction; too hard to set up . . . We watched it a long time, for it was most interesting, most fascinating, but it was not practical—that to me was clear.

The Paige typesetter had failed the trial, and Rogers told Twain that the machine had no further commercial potential. Twain had a hard time accepting the news, and for several weeks kept making suggestions about how the machine might still work. Finally, he had to accept that the investment he had been counting on for years was worthless, and that he still had serious financial problems.

Troubling Times

While Twain was in the midst of his dealing with Paige, neither Twain nor Rogers realized how near Twain's publishing firm, Charles L. Webster and Company, was to collapsing. The bank refused any more credit, and on April 18, 1894, the company declared bankruptcy. Fortunately, prior to the bankruptcy, Twain had given power of attorney to Rogers, who assigned all of Twain's copyrights to Livy.

Although the bankruptcy agreement was to settle the other $100,000 debt at fifty cents on the dollar, Twain vowed to repay the entire amount. Bankruptcy shamed both Twain and Livy, who agreed with her husband that every cent be paid.

Twain persuaded the American Publishing Company to pick up *Puddn'head Wilson* for subscription publication. Although sales were modest, initial reviews were mostly complimentary. Critic Leslie Fiedler claimed that the book was "morally . . . one of the most honest books in our literature." However, the *Athenaeum*, on January 19, 1895, complained that "the story at times rambles on in an almost incomprehensible way." Recent critics have studied the novel more in regard to the questions it raises about racial identity and to what Twain was trying to say about racism.

Twain had also arranged with *Harper's Monthly Magazine* to serialize his book on Joan of Arc when it was completed. They agreed to pay him $75 per page. Twain insisted that they publish it anonymously because he feared that if people saw his name, they would be disappointed when they found nothing humorous. Within the work, Twain hid his identity as its creator through layers of fictional narrators and interpreters: the story is told by the aged Sieur Louis de Conte, secretary of Joan of Arc, and translated by Jean François Alden.

He returned to Europe in August 1894 and resumed work. By December he had moved to working on the second part of the book concerning Joan's military feats. In February he began the third part about her trial. This was the most difficult because of the historical accuracy required.

However, his work was slowed as his worries about his debts continued to consume him. He decided the quickest way to pay them off was to return to the lecture circuit. Twain told Rogers, who continued to give financial advice: "Apparently, I've *got* to mount the platform next fall or starve." Twain believed he could travel around the world, giving lectures while at the same time gathering material for a new book.

Twain's family had stabilized in the previous few years. Livy was stronger than she had been for several years, and Susy seemed less agitated about the separation from her best friend. Clara continued a musical career, and Jean suffered only minor fainting spells, not the previous seizures. They returned to Quarry Farm to plan Twain's world tour.

While there, Twain put the finishing touches to *Personal Recollections of Joan of Arc*, which he read aloud each night to his family. Susy especially identified with Joan, perhaps because her father had used her as a model for Joan's physical appearance. Susy frequently had to leave the room to get a handkerchief for her tears. After the last night's reading, Susy said: "To-night Joan of Arc was buried at the stake." The book was completed and Twain sent it to *Harper's Monthly*. He told H. H. Rogers: "Possibly the book may not sell, but that is nothing—it was written for love."

As the date of Twain's world tour approached, it was decided that Susy would stay in America with her Aunt Susan, Katy Leary, and little sister Jean, while Livy and Clara would accompany Twain. They left Elmira on July 14, 1895, and Twain began his tour in Cleveland, Ohio. He traveled through the northern United States and Canada, doing readings over a span of thirty-three days.

When he departed from New York in late August to begin his tour abroad, Twain emphasized to reporters that all the proceeds from his lectures were going to the clearing of his debts. Twain traveled through Australia, New Zealand, India, and South America, receiving an enthusiastic welcome wherever he spoke. However, throughout the tour he suffered from a pus-filled carbuncle the size of a turkey egg on his left leg and from continued bouts with colds.

Back in the United States, with the serialization of *Joan of Arc* completed, the publishing company Harper & Brothers published the novel in book form. Unlike with its magazine publication, Mark Twain's name appeared on the work.

Be good + you will be lonesome.

Mark Twain

Twain reclining on a ship's deck in 1896 *(Courtesy of Yale Collection of American Literature, Beinecke Rare Book and Manuscript Library)*

Critics were not enthusiastic about Twain's latest effort. Many felt that he should have stayed with his usual style, and they failed to give the book much in-depth consideration. Most agreed that the strongest part was the fifteen chapters in Book Three about Joan's trial for heresy. This disturbed Twain, who, to insure accuracy, had copied almost verbatim the translated Latin transcripts of that historical event. Another criticism was that Joan seemed as though she belonged more in the nineteenth century than in the fifteenth when she lived.

Even Twain's friend and critic, William Dean Howells, who usually was one of Twain's biggest admirers, had mixed

MARK TWAIN'S
JOAN of ARC

HARPER & BROTHERS
PUBLISHERS

Twain's *Joan of Arc* received lukewarm reviews when it was published.
(Library of Congress)

feelings about the work. In a review in *Harper's Weekly*, Howells wrote:

> I am not at all troubled when he comes out with a bit of good, strong, downright modern American feeling; my suffering begins when he does the supposed medieval thing. Then I suspect that his armor is of tin, that the castles and rocks are paste-board, that the mob of citizens and soldiers who fill the air with the clash of their two-up-and-two-down combats, and the well-known muffled roar of their voices have been hired in at so much a night, and that Joan is sometimes in an awful temper behind the scenes . . . But, in spite of all this, the book has a

William Dean Howells *(Library of Congress)*

vitalizing force. Joan lives in it again, and dies, and then lives on in the love and pity and wonder of the reader.

Friend and critic Brandon Matthews tried to place the blame on Twain's having chosen a poor genre: "Mark Twain as a historical novelist is not at his best . . . the historical novel is an outworn anachronism."

Twain, on the other hand, considered the book his best and the only one that he thought good enough to dedicate to his beloved wife Livy. In 1908, reflecting on his life's works, Twain wrote: "I like the *Joan of Arc* best of all my books; & it *is* the best; I know it perfectly well. And besides, it furnished me seven times the pleasure afforded me by any of the others: 12 years of preparation & 2 years of writing. The others needed no preparation, & got none."

Exactly one year from the time they had left Elmira on Twain's world tour, Twain and his family headed to England, where Katy Leary planned to bring Susy and Jean to join their parents and Clara. Upon arrival in England, they received a letter from Katy stating that Susy was too ill to travel. Livy and Clara decided to return to America immediately, leaving Twain behind to work on his writing. Three days after they sailed on August 19, 1896, Twain received news of the death of his daughter Susy. She had suffered a high temperature leading to delirium and blindness. Her illness was diagnosed as spinal meningitis, a type of brain infection.

Livy and Clara were still at sea and received the news of Susy's death when the captain handed them a message that read: "MARK TWAIN'S ELDEST DAUGHTER DIES OF SPINAL MENINGITIS." At first Livy refused to believe the news. Later she began to brood and read poems about death.

Twain tried to block out his sadness, playing endless billiard games. He and Livy never spoke to each other about their grief.

But the loss of Susy had staggered Twain. Susy was the child most like her father and his favorite. He wrote to his friend, the Reverend Joe Twichell: "I did know that Susy was part of us; I did *not* know that she could go away . . . and take our lives with her." As he did many years earlier when his brother died and again with his son, Twain blamed himself

After the death of his favorite daughter, Susy, Twain played billiards to escape from his grief. *(Library of Congress)*

for Susy's death, believing that if he had not brought on their financial problems, the family would not have been separated when Susy first became ill. A year after Susy's death, Twain wrote a long poem called "In Memoriam," which had a healing effect for Twain. *Harper's Monthly* published the verse in the November edition.

After Susy's burial, the rest of the family went into seclusion in London. Twain continued to work hard to pay off his debts but took time out to assist a blind and deaf girl, Helen Keller, by securing money to send her to college. Twain had first met Helen when she was fourteen years old, and he immediately admired her resolve to be educated despite her handicaps. Since that time, Keller had passed the entrance exam to Radcliffe College. Twain introduced Helen to Henry Rogers and his wife, and appealed to the couple to contact some of their wealthy friends to raise enough money to establish a college fund for Keller. They collected sufficient money to pay for Keller's college education.

In New York a report that Twain and his family were living in poverty in London surfaced. The *New York Herald* began a fund for people to donate. One article suggested that the family's lack of funds was due to a medical condition afflicting Twain. The truth was that a cousin of Twain's, James Ross Clemens, was seriously ill. But the media saw the Clemens name and mistakenly reported that Samuel Clemens (Twain) was dead or dying. This caused Twain to cable a New York reporter this statement: "The report of my illness grew out of his illness; the report of my death was an exaggeration."

Despite all his problems—finances, Susy's death, and Jean suffering from more and more frequent epileptic seizures—Twain continued his work and his normal activities. The fam-

Twain helped establish a college fund for Helen Keller (above). *(Library of Congress)*

ily went to Switzerland for the summer, but Twain returned to London to report for several American newspapers on Queen Victoria's 1897 Diamond Jubilee, commemorating her sixty-year reign. Twain began to feel new enthusiasm for his writing and completed *Following the Equator: A Journey Around the World*, the story of his last lecture tour. In this fifth and last travel book, Twain makes no pretense about who is telling the story.

Although some humor appears, the story for the most part is more serious than his previous travel books, covering social, political, and economic issues of some of the countries visited. Each chapter heading has a saying from Puddn'head Wilson's Calendar, such as the one found at the beginning of Chapter Two: *"Adam was but human—this explains it all. He did not want the apple for the apple's sake; he wanted it only because it was forbidden. The mistake was in not forbidding the serpent; then he would have eaten the serpent."*

In December Twain received a cable notifying him of the death of his seventy-three-year-old brother Orion. Twain had not seen his brother in a decade, and they had not even corresponded since Twain and his family moved to Europe. Although Twain sent his sister-in-law fifty dollars for funeral costs and fifty dollars a month thereafter to help with expenses, he expressed no emotion about his brother's death, at least not in writing.

On a brighter note, by January Twain's royalties had finally paid off his debts. To celebrate, he took his family to Vienna, where he hoped to get better medical care for Jean. While in Vienna, sixty-seven-year-old Theodor Leschetizky, a famous Austrian piano teacher, accepted Clara as a pupil. During her lessons, she met another of Leschetizky's students,

Ossip Gabrilowitsch, whom she married ten years later. The entire family wanted to return to their home in Hartford and made plans to do so in the spring of 1899 after Clara finished her piano lessons. Politics also prompted a quick departure from Austria: the Spanish-American War had broken out, and America's invasion of Cuba was not popular with Europeans.

Twain continued to write, producing shorter works, such as the story "The Man That Corrupted Hadleyburg." The story is about a town that thrives on its reputation for being honest and upright, always able to shun temptation. However, its virtue comes from its isolation—no temptation is ever allowed to enter the village. Because they do not want any outsiders to corrupt them, the townspeople mistreat a stranger who passes through the town. A vindictive, revengeful soul, the stranger decides to get even by destroying their arrogance about being incorruptible. By drawing all of the so-called honest people into a scheme to get wealthy, he brings about the downfall of the entire town.

By this point in his life, Twain had sufficient money in the bank, no longer owed on the Hartford house and furnishings, and received generous royalties from his American and British copyrights. The family stayed in Vienna until May 1899 and then left for London. Twain told reporters that the family hoped to return to the United States before winter.

At about the same time, Clara made a sudden decision to drop piano lessons. With her small delicate hands inherited from her father, she could not reach the keys adequately. She announced that she wanted to become a concert singer and that she could take lessons in either London or New York. For some time Jean had been receiving treatments for her epilepsy that the family believed she could get only in Europe. After Twain learned that the treatments were also available in the United States, they sailed for New York in October 1900.

After eight years abroad and Susy's death in the Hartford house, they did not want to go back to Connecticut and planned to settle in New York. New Yorkers greeted Twain enthusiastically, and invitations for public appearances overwhelmed him. Twain and William Dean Howells renewed their friendship. Since Howells had also lost a daughter, the two comforted each other. Twain's problem with his writing hand convinced him that his days of composing entire books were over, but he could still write articles for magazines. No longer needing money, he turned down a generous offer for a lecture tour.

Twain and Livy decided to sell the Hartford house after Twain had passed by it one day as he was returning from a funeral. He remarked: "If we ever enter the house to live our hearts will break." They advertised the house at $60,000—fifty thousand below its value according to Twain—but no buyers showed an interest. Ever cautious about money, Livy did not want them to buy a house in New York until they sold the house in Connecticut. They settled temporarily in a rented house on West Tenth Street, where a steady stream of people visited them. Twain received so many invitations to dinner and to speak that he started arriving too late to eat but just in time to speak.

With all of his after-dinner talks, and his ability to speak on almost any topic, Americans began to view Twain as the country's philosopher. Most agreed with him on such definitions as the one he gave for a classic: "Something everybody wants to have read and nobody wants to read." In the fall of

Twain with Livy (center) and daughter Clara at their suburban
London home in 1900 *(Courtesy of AP Images)*

1901, Yale awarded him an honorary Doctor of Letters degree. He became involved in politics; as he spoke out against Tammany Hall and "Boss" Richard Croker, Twain urged a clean city government and police reform. His speeches figured largely in the ensuing change that came to New York City government.

In May, Twain and Livy finally bought another home, this time in Tarrytown, New York. The next month Twain accepted a Doctor of Letters degree from the University of Missouri. The trip to receive this award was the last time Twain saw Hannibal, the scene of his youth. While in Hannibal, Twain visited the graves of his parents and younger brother Henry. He later wrote: "Almost every tombstone recorded a forgotten name that had been familiar and pleasant to my ear when I was a boy there fifty years before." He paid a last visit to St. Louis, where he participated in ground-breaking ceremonies for the 1904 World's Fair that commemorated Lewis and Clark's expedition. He also helped rededicate a steamboat as

the "Mark Twain."

While Twain was receiving these honors, Livy and Jean went for the summer to a cottage in York Harbor, Maine. Clara was still in Europe, studying music. Almost immediately after they arrived at

Richard Croker
(Library of Congress)

the cottage, Jean had a major seizure. Then Livy's many physical ailments returned. By early August she was seriously ill and had trouble breathing. Two doctors provided twenty-four hour care.

Clara returned to the United States, hoping her presence would be good for her mother. Katy Leary cared for Livy, who was so weak that she could sit up only ten minutes a day. In September, after suffering a relapse, Livy begged to go home, where she improved slightly. Nevertheless, her condition required round-the-clock care provided by Katy, Clara, and a special nurse.

When Jean became ill for a month with pneumonia, she was bedridden and required constant attention. The family had to create excuses for Livy's not hearing Jean moving about the house. Months passed before doctors allowed Twain to see his wife. They feared that in his anxiety, he would blurt out information about Jean's condition or other news that would send Livy's blood pressure dangerously high. When Twain finally got a chance to visit Livy, his time in the sickroom was limited to five minutes or less.

As usual, Twain blamed himself for the sad situation. He believed that the financial problems and the shame of the Webster and Company bankruptcy, even though by now all the creditors had been paid, had caused Livy such deep distress that she became ill. Since he could not visit Livy, he hired Isabel Lyons to be her secretary and to help out in any other ways she was needed.

Although Twain accepted the time restraints on his visits with his wife, he missed Livy. In fact, he was a lonely man, as Jean kept to herself and Clara was busy caring for her mother and continuing her singing lessons. Since he could not see Livy very often, he wrote notes to her twice a day. In a note he could be sure that he did not reveal any bad news that might harm her health. In the spring doctors suggested a warmer climate would benefit Livy. Twain sold their house in New York, and the family spent the summer at Quarry Farm, where Livy slowly grew stronger.

Henry Rogers made arrangements in October to transfer the publication of all of Twain's books—past, present, and future—to Harper & Brothers publishers with a guaranteed $25,000 annual income for five years. This was a minimum as his books often brought in twice that much. With no money problems, Twain concentrated on getting Livy well. To that end, he made arrangements to take her to the warmer climate of Florence, Italy, where they had enjoyed a previous visit. They sailed in October, accompanied by Katy Leary, a nurse, Isabel Lyons, and Isabel's mother.

The situation was not what they had expected. The house that Twain rented, sight unseen, was a fifty-room palace called the Villa de Quarto. The place was run by a hostile landlady, and the sunny weather for which they had hoped was instead cold and dismal. With Twain's visits now limited to two minutes each day, he missed Livy even more. Sometimes he sneaked into her room for just a few more minutes with her. Katy Leary reported that Livy would "put her arms around his neck the first thing, and he'd hold her soft, and give her one of them tender kisses . . . It was a love that was more than earthly love—it was heavenly."

By January 1904 Livy showed a definite improvement in her health, and in February the couple celebrated their thirty-third wedding anniversary. After finishing some articles for *Harper's Monthly*, Twain began work on his autobiography, which he planned as a series of memory fragments in no chronological order. Because he did not intend for the autobiography to be published in his lifetime, he was completely candid in what he wrote.

Livy's improved health did not last, and she alternated good days with bad ones. However, by early June she seemed so much better that one evening Twain started talking about building their own villa in Italy. In the excitement of those plans, Twain visited with Livy much longer than usual. He left her room to let Katy Leary get Livy ready for bed and started playing on the piano some of the spirituals he remembered from his childhood. Just as he stopped playing, Katy lifted Livy's head from the pillow, and Livy died almost instantly in Katy's arms. Twain did not know that his wife had died until he went back to tell her goodnight. Around her bed he found his daughters and Katy standing as if in trances.

To his friend Joe Twichell, Twain described the sight of Livy when he first saw her body: "How sweet she was in death, how young, how beautiful, how like her dear girlish self of thirty years ago, not a gray hair showing!" However, to his friend William Dean Howells, he revealed the depth of his sorrow: "I am tired & old; I wish I were with Livy."

Twain and his two daughters returned to the United States to bury Livy in the family plot. Joe Twichell, who had married Livy and Twain thirty-four years earlier, performed the funeral on July 14 at the old Langdon home in Elmira. Twain placed a simple marker at Livy's grave to show her name, dates of her birth and death, and this epitaph in German: "Got sei dir gnädig, O meine Wonne!" (God be merciful to thee, Oh, my Rapture)

Life's tragedies continued to plague the Clemens family. Daughter Clara, who had faithfully assisted during her mother's twenty-two month illness, suffered a nervous breakdown. She spent almost a year in a New York sanitarium, resting and recovering. Her younger sister Jean, who was enjoying a respite from her many illnesses, was injured while riding horseback with friends. Something spooked her horse, and it ran into a trolley car, knocking Jean temporarily unconscious and killing the horse. Although Jean also suffered broken bones in her ankle and severe bruising, she did recover. In September, Twain received news of the death of his sister Pamela.

Twain decided to settle in New York again and moved into a house on Fifth Avenue. Twain leased the large house for $3,000 a month, and he brought out of storage the Hartford house furniture that he had not seen for thirteen years in order to provide a comfortable home for his daughters. Neither of them ever spent any extended amount of time there with him, though. Although Katy Leary and Jean resided at that address, Jean spent most of her days in a small cottage on the property, where she carved wooden animal figures. Clara recovered from her breakdown and resumed voice lessons.

EIGHT

Halley's Comet Comes Again

In 1905 Harper & Brothers recognized Twain's seventieth birthday with an elaborate party at which each guest received a twelve-inch plaster bust of the honoree. Despite the warm wishes and a standing ovation, Twain had a hard time shaking the melancholy that gripped him. He later described such despair in the closing chapter of "The Mysterious Stranger," a short story on which he had worked for years to develop the theme of the blurred boundaries between good and evil: "there is no God, no universe, no human race, no earthly life, no heaven, no hell. It is all a dream—a grotesque and foolish dream. Nothing exists but you. And you are but a *thought*—a vagrant thought, a useless thought, a homeless thought, wandering forlorn among the empty eternities!" The work was not published until a number of years after Twain's death. Throughout 1906, Twain tried to distract himself from his weariness, speaking at such

Twain (left) and his party sitting around a dining table at Delmonico's Restaurant in New York City to celebrate his seventieth birthday. *(Courtesy of the Museum of the City of New York/Byron Collection/Getty Images)*

benefits as one for the San Francisco earthquake victims and at a fund raiser for Tuskegee Institute, a college founded by a slave owner and a slave. That same year, Twain selected Alfred Bigelow Paine as his official biographer. When Harper & Brothers offered Twain a large amount of money to publish excerpts from his autobiography in the *North American Review*, Twain reversed his decision that none of the work could be published in his lifetime. He chose five 10,000-word selections, mostly about his childhood and youth, to be included in the magazine. Although he enjoyed the additional income, Twain did not plan to write anything else of a major nature. He spent much of each day playing billiards, especially after his friend Henry Rogers gave him a billiard table

Twain playing pool with his biographer, Alfred Paine. *(Courtesy of New York Public Library)*

for Christmas. Twain taught his biographer Paine to play, and the two established a close friendship.

However, recurring bad dreams plagued Twain. Despite his current stable financial situation, he had nightmares about returning to poverty and having to become a river boat pilot again. He also had dreams of being on the lecture circuit trying to be humorous, having no one laugh, and then seeing the audience walk out. In a third nightmare he attended a fancy social occasion in his night clothes. Everyone stared, and he felt ashamed. All of these dreams of inadequacy made him restless. A sense of darkness taking over his life was increased when Jean, in the course of a violent epileptic seizure, tried to kill her caretaker, Katy Leary. Twain had to place Jean in a sanitarium.

At Paine's urging, Twain decided to leave New York and build a new home on a 248-acre plot in Redding, Connecticut. He believed the five excerpts from his autobiography would cover the cost of the house. Twain hired John Mead Howells, the son of his old friend William Dean Howells, to design and build the house with two stipulations: the cost must not exceed $25,000 and Twain did not want to see it until it was finished, furnished, and ready to move in.

In June 1907 Twain received notice that Oxford University planned to bestow on him a doctoral degree. Twain eagerly accepted the honor and traveled to London for the ceremony.

Twain dressed in his Oxford robe *(Library of Congress)*

In 1907, Twain decided to wear only white suits. *(Library of Congress)*

Clad in the scarlet robes of the British university, Twain could scarcely believe that someone like him, with little formal education, had received such an accolade. He was so proud that he wore the scarlet robes on a number of occasions.

Upon returning to the United States, Twain spoke to a Congressional hearing on copyright laws. Despite its being winter, Twain appeared before the Congressmen dressed all in white, including his shoes. He later asked reporters: "Why don't you ask why I am wearing such apparently unseasonable cloths? I'll tell you. I have found that when a man reaches the advanced age of seventy-one years as I have, the continual sight of dark clothing is likely to have a depressing effect upon him. Light-colored clothing is more pleasing to the eye and enlivens the spirit." Twain liked the look so much that from then on, he wore only white suits year round. He called the new look "my don'tcareadam" suit.

In early 1908 Twain made two trips to Bermuda. There he met Margaret Blackmer, a child whom he unofficially adopted as a granddaughter. Playing games with her reminded him of earlier days when he entertained his daughters. To re-create those happy years and to compensate for his loneliness, Twain began to write letters to other young girls that he met. He established a club in which, at age seventy-three, he was the only male member. He referred to the girls as "angelfish" after a beautiful fish he had seen in Bermuda, and he called the group the Aquarium. During the remainder of his life, he invited over a dozen girls into membership in the club and always carried with him several of their club's emblems, a small enamel angelfish pin, so that he could welcome a new member immediately.

In June Twain moved into his new house at Redding. Daughter Clara and his personal secretary Isabel Lyon had overseen all the decorations. Although he had taken no part in the house's construction or furnishing, he was delighted when he did see it: "It is a perfect house—perfect, so far as I can see, in every detail." He later named the house "Stormfield" after the captain in his short story, "Captain Stormfield's Visit to Heaven." The sale of that work had helped him finish paying for the eighteen-room house that eventually cost $60,000.

Twain standing with Dorothy Quick, one of his angelfish girls, in 1907.
(Library of Congress)

Sometimes Twain invited one or more of the angelfish girls and their mothers to be his houseguests. He claimed that one of the reasons for building Stormfield was to have a place for them to stay when they came for a visit. He designated the billiard room as the club's official headquarters and hung pictures of the girls all around the room. He gave "fish" names, such as "The Fish Market," to other parts of the house. Yearning to keep in touch with the girls, Twain threatened to suspend from the club anyone who did not write to him at least once in a three-month period. After finally hearing from one of the young ladies who had not written in some time, Twain wrote to her:

> At last, you dear little tardy rascal! This morning I was going to stick up a notice on the back porch:
>
> LOST CHILD
>
> --
>
> --
>
> Answers to the name of Dorothy.
>
> --
>
> --
>
> Strayed, Stolen or Mislaid.
>
> DISAPPEARED
>
> On or about the 9th of August.
>
> --
>
> --
>
> Any one restoring this inestimably
>
> precious asset to the
>
> SORROWING
>
> Will be richly
>
> REWARDED!

The girls enjoyed his letters to them just as much and expressed their disappointment when he did not write as often as they would like. The same Dorothy wrote to him:

"I have been watching the mail for a long while expecting a letter every day I feel very lonesome for you when you dont write for so long Mother says you are a very busy man and I should have patience but I cant." Some three hundred such letters between Twain and the angelfish girls were published in *Mark Twain's Aquarium: The Samuel Clemens Angelfish Correspondence.*

Twain spent most of his time alone at Stormfield, vacillating between good moods and bad ones. When companions like Henry Rogers visited, Twain was friendly and sociable. When he did not feel good, he usually took out his bad mood on his devoted secretary, Isabel Lyon, who so adored him that she never complained. She did avail herself of his Scotch whiskey to settle her nerves.

Clara stayed away from her father as much as possible while she continued her musical career. Jean, who was still in the sanitarium, begged her father to let her come home. He refused, telling her that he and the doctor knew what was best for her. Jean could not accept that her father did not want her to come home and in her mind blamed his secretary whom she believed did not want to share Twain's attention.

In August 1908 Twain learned that his sister's son, Samuel E. Moffett, had drowned on a New Jersey beach. Twain had always been especially fond of this nephew and traveled, despite the heat, to New York for the funeral. Upon return to Stormfield, Twain became ill with dizziness and slight loss of memory. Although he recovered within a few days, doctors later said that it was the beginning of more serious illness.

Just three months after moving into Stormfield, burglars carried off several bundles of silver. Claude, the butler, fired a shot to scare them off, and the local police soon picked them up. The two later received harsh sentences. Twain posted the following notice on his front door:

NOTICE TO THE NEXT BURGLAR

There is nothing but plated ware in this house now and

henceforth.

You will find it in that brass thing in the dining-room over in the corner by the basket of kittens.

If you want the basket put the kittens in the brass thing.

Do not make a noise—it disturbs the family.

You will find rubbers in the front hall by that thing which has the umbrellas in it, chiffonnier, I think they call it, or pergola, or something like that.

Please close the door when you go away!

Very truly yours,

S. L. Clemens

Clara took over management of Stormfield and convinced her father to get rid of the two servants who had long served him faithfully. Then she began urging her father to allow Jean to return home. With Clara's manipulation, Twain decided that his long-time secretary, Isabel Lyon, not he, had been the one to reject Jean's previous pleas to come home. He wrote to his daughter: "Dear child, you will be as welcome as if it were your mother herself calling you home from exile!"

Jean returned home in spring 1909, apparently much improved in health. Clara, aided by Paine, continued to undermine Isabel Lyon and finally convinced Twain that she had been stealing from him for years. Twain fired her and told Clara that Lyon was "a liar, a forger, a thief, a hypocrite, a drunkard, a sneak, a humbug, a traitor, a conspirator."

In May, Twain went to New York to visit Henry Rogers. Clara, who was in New York at the time, met her father at the train station to tell him that his friend had just died of a stroke. The news greatly upset Twain, who served as a pall bearer at the funeral but could not go watch his friend be buried.

With Jean home, Clara started spending more time at Stormfield, and for the first time in many years, Twain did not feel lonely. In June, Twain went to Baltimore to speak to the senior class of St. Timothy's, a girls' school from which one of his angelfish was graduating. He almost immediately fell ill from the heat, the exertion, and the humidity. He complained of pains in his chest but tried to convince himself that it was only indigestion.

Back at Stormfield, his doctor diagnosed his problem as heart disease and recommended complete bed rest and no more cigar smoking. Twain refused to give up his beloved cigars, even though they were killing him. He also ignored the complete bed rest order and by September walked and played billiards regularly. However, he confided to his friends that he was dying: "I came in with Halley's comet in 1835. It is coming again next year, and I expect to go out with it."

On October 6, 1909, daughter Clara married concert pianist Ossip Gabrilowitsch, whom she had known for a decade. Only family and a few friends attended the ceremony performed by Joe Twichell. At his daughter's request Twain wore his scarlet Oxford robes over his white suit. When asked if he were happy about the marriage, Twain replied: "Yes, fully as much as any marriage could please me or any other father. There are two or three solemn things in life and a happy marriage is one of them, for the terrors of life are all to come. I am glad of this marriage, and Mrs. Clemens would be glad, for she always had a warm affection for Gabrilowitsch."

Clara and her new husband planned to live in Europe but were delayed a month in their departure when Ossip had to have surgery for appendicitis. When they finally left the United States, neither Clara nor Twain knew that she was pregnant with Twain's only grandchild.

Twain was well enough to go to Bermuda again in November and spent his seventy-fourth birthday there. He completed the last article he ever wrote for publication, "The Turning Point of My Life," a statement of his general philosophy that there was no one turning point in his life but rather a chain of thousands of links. Twain believed that writing was the most important aspect of his life, so the first link was the one that turned him in that direction—his youthful apprenticeship to a printer.

Throughout the essay he names other important links: finding the $50 bill that allowed him to go down the Mississippi to New Orleans, where he planned to leave for South America. Since there were no ships leaving any time soon, he became a river boat pilot. Then the Civil War brought that job to an end, and he headed West with his brother Orion. The essay continues in this vein, enumerating all the other incidents that made up the chain of his becoming a literary man. Twain concluded: "Each event has its own place in the eternal chain of circumstances, and whether it be big or little it will infallibly cause the *next* event."

Twain decided to go back to New York for the Christmas holidays but was disappointed when he arrived to find headlines about his poor health. At home he complained to his daughter Jean who called in Twain's response to the newspapers: "I hear the newspapers say I am dying. The charge is not true. I would not do such a thing at my time of life. I am behaving as good as I can. Merry Christmas to everybody!"

But another monumental loss struck Twain on Christmas Eve: Jean drowned in the bathtub after suffering an epileptic seizure. Katy Leary had waited outside the bathroom door while Jean bathed. When she did not appear after some time, Katy knocked on the door. Getting no response, Katy entered the bathroom and found Jean dead. The next day, Jean's body, clad in the dress she had worn at her sister's wedding, was carried from the house in a snowstorm, as her father watched from a window. He could not bear to attend the funeral, after which she was buried next to her mother and her sister Susy. Despite his grief, a few days later, Twain acknowledged his relief at Jean's release from pain.

On New Year's Day Twain decided to go to Bermuda, even though his chest pain had returned. This time Claude, his butler, accompanied him. Twain's health prevented his participation in many activities, and he still suffered from heart spasms. He had a severe bronchitis attack in February and the next month decided that he should return home. Before he did so, Paine received a letter from the parents of one of Twain's angelfish, describing the worsening of Twain's health. Paine left to go bring Twain home and also called Clara and her husband to come back from Europe. On the way home Twain suffered several attacks and had to be carried from the ship. Although Twain knew he was dying, he remained calm and showed appreciation to all who cared for him.

Clara and Ossip arrived on April 14. By now Clara was obviously pregnant, but Twain did not seem to notice because of the drugs given to him for pain. Halley's Comet appeared in the sky on April 20, 1910, although it would not reach its most spectacular appearance for another two weeks. The next morning Twain had trouble speaking, although his mind was clear enough to understand others. In the early afternoon he reached for Clara's hand and went into a deep sleep. He died peacefully at sunset on April 21, whispering to Clara: "Goodbye dear, if we meet---."

His body was placed for viewing in Brick Church in Manhattan, where huge crowds passed by his coffin. Then he was buried near all of his loved ones—wife Livy, daughters Susy and Jean, and little son, Langdon, at Woodlawn Cemetery in Elmira, New York. Clara and Ossip remained at Stormfield, along with Katy Leary, until August when Clara gave birth to their daughter Nina, Twain's only descendant.

William Dean Howells paid final tribute to his good friend shortly after Twain's death. Howells said: "I looked a moment at the face I knew so well; and it was patient with the patience I had so often seen in it; something of a puzzle, a great silent dignity, an assent to what must be from the depths of a nature whose tragical seriousness broke in the laughter which the unwise took for the whole of him." The great writer was silenced, gone from the earth on the tail of another Halley's Comet. Behind he left a reputation aptly summarized by Howells, who concluded : "Clemens was sole, incomparable, the Lincoln of our literature."

Timeline

1835    Samuel Langhorne Clemens born November 30, in Florida, Missouri. Halley's comet visible from Earth.

1839    Family settles in Hannibal, Missouri.

1847   Father, John Marshall Clemens, dies.

1848   Starts newspaper apprenticeship.

1850   Goes to work as printer at brother Orion's newspaper.

1853   Leaves home for St. Louis.

1857    Travels to New Orleans, hoping to go to South America; starts cub pilot apprenticeship.

1858   Brother Henry killed in steamboat explosion.

1861   Joins Marion Rangers; goes to Nevada with
        brother Orion.

1862    Joins staff of *Virginia City
        Daily Territorial Enterprise*.

1863   First uses pseudonym "Mark Twain."

1864   Leaves Nevada for San Francisco; works for
        San Francisco Morning Call.

1865   "The Celebrated Jumping Frog
        of Calaveras County" published
        in New York.

1866   Tours Sandwich Islands and writes travel letters
        for *San Francisco Union*; sends scoop on *Hornet*
        disaster at sea to *Union*; gives lecture, leading to
        first tour.

1867   Tours Holy Land and Europe as part of *Quaker
        City* pilgrimage; works in Washington, D.C., for
        Senator William M. Stewart of Nevada; gathers
        material for *The Gilded Age*; meets Olivia
        Langdon.

1869  Begins seventy-lecture tour to make money in order to marry Olivia; publishes *The Innocents Abroad*.

1870 Marries Olivia on February 2; son Langdon born prematurely.

1872 Publishes *Roughing It*; daughter Olivia Susan (Susy) born on March 19; son Langdon dies on June 2.

1873  Publishes *The Gilded Age*; patents self-pasting scrapbook.

1874 Daughter Clara born on June 8.

1876 Publishes *The Adventures of Tom Sawyer*.

1880 Publishes *A Tramp Abroad*; daughter Jane Lampton (Jean) born on July 26.

1881 Publishes *The Prince and the Pauper.*

1883 Publishes *Life on the Mississippi.*

1884 Founds publishing company, Charles L. Webster & Company.

1885  Publishes *The Adventures of Huckleberry Finn*; contracts to publish *Personal Memoirs of Ulysses S. Grant.*

1889 Publishes *A Connecticut Yankee in King Arthur's Court.*

1890 Mother, Jane Lampton Clemens, dies October 27; invests in Paige typesetter.

1891 Moves to Europe.

1894  Charles L. Webster and Company goes bankrupt; publishes *The Tragedy of Puddn'head Wilson.*

1895	Begins worldwide lecture tour; publishes *Personal Recollections of Joan of Arc.*
1896	Daughter Susy dies on August 18.
1897	Publishes *Following the Equator.*
1901	Accepts honorary degree from Yale University.
1903	Negotiates contract with Harper & Brothers to become sole publishers of Twain's works; moves to Italy for Livy's health.
1904	Livy dies on June 5 in Florence, Italy.
1907	Accepts honorary degree from Oxford.
1908	Moves into Stormfield; organizes Angelfish Club.
1909	Daughter Clara marries Ossip Gabrilowitsch on October 6; daughter Jean drowns in bathtub on December 23.

1910 "I came in with Halley's comet in 1835... I expect to go out with it:" Dies on April 21, the day after the comet came into earth's view; buried in Woodlawn Cemetery in Elmira, New York; granddaughter, Nina Gabrilowitsch, born on August 18.

Sources

CHAPTER ONE: Family Ties

p. 11, "unfettered and entirely . . ." DeLancey Ferguson, *Mark Twain: Man and Legend* (New York: The Bobbs-Merrill Company, Inc., 1963), 49.

p. 14, "My father and I . . ." E. Hudson Long, *Mark Twain Handbook* (New York: Hendricks House, 1957), 92.

p. 14, "All through my boyhood . . ." Dixon Wecter, *Sam Clemens of Hannibal* (Cambridge, MA: The Riverside Press, 1952), 19-20.

p. 15, "Whatever befalls me . . ." Albert Bigelow Paine, *Mark Twain* (New York: Chelsea House, 1980), 1:6.

p. 15, "I've looked out for *them* . . ." Mark Twain and Charles Dudley Warner, *The Gilded Age: A Tale of Today* (New York: A Meridian Book, 1994), 26-27.

p. 16, "The dog has a tail . . ." Samuel Charles Webster, *Mark Twain: Business Man* (Boston: Little, Brown and Company, 1946), 44.

p. 18, "I suppose that during . . ." Mark Twain, *Mark Twain's Autobiography* (New York: P. F. Collier and Son and Company, 1925), 1:108.

p. 18, "He drives me crazy . . ." Paine, *Mark Twain*, 1:35.

p. 19, "In all my life . . ." Bernard De Voto, ed., *Mark Twain in Eruption* (New York: Grosset & Dunlap, Publishers, 1940), 109.

p. 20, "Then we said it was . . ." Mark Twain, *The Innocents Abroad or The New Pilgrims Progress* (New York: New American Library, 1966), 457.

p. 20, "My own knowledge . . ." Fred Kaplan, *The Singular Mark Twain* (New York: Doubleday, 2003), 16.

p. 20, "It was on the farm . . ." Twain, *Autobiography*, 1:100.

p. 21, "W-h-a-r-r's my golden . . ." Paine, *Mark Twain*, 1:15.

p. 22, "You've got it!" Ibid., 16.

p. 22, "*and she tore him* . . ." Ibid.

p. 22, "to make them understand . . ." Ron Powers, *Mark*

Twain: A Life (New York: Free Press, 2005), 320.
p. 23, "If Christ were here . . ." Ibid., 29.
p. 23, "inquiring into matters . . ." Mark Twain, *1601, and Is Shakespeare Dead?* (New York: Oxford University Press, 1996), 21.
p. 23, "that it was a holy . . ." Twain, *Autobiography*, 1:101.
p. 23, "We were comrades . . ." Ibid., 100.
p. 23, "Poor thing, when he . . ." Ibid., 102.

CHAPTER TWO: Apprenticeship
p. 25, "I do not now know . . ." Twain, *Autobiography*, 2:185.
p. 27, "a long, dusky, shapeless . . ." Twain, *The Innocents Abroad*, 126-127.
p. 27, "never smoke more than . . ." Milton Meltzer, *Mark Twain Himself* (New York: Wings Books, 1993), 12.
p. 27, "He was the only really . . ." Twain, *Autobiography*, 2:174.
p. 28, "Cling to the land . . ." Paine, *Mark Twain*, 1:73
p. 28, "Oh mother, I will do . . ." Powers, *Mark Twain: A Life*, 43.
p. 31, "One isn't a printer . . ." Ferguson, *Mark Twain: Man and Legend*, 35.
p. 36, "I want you to repeat . . ." Paine, *Mark Twain*, 1:93.
p. 40, "his feelings so much overcame . . ." Edward Wagenkecht, *Mark Twain: The Man and His Work,* 3rd ed. (Norman, OK: University of Oklahoma Press, 1967), 11.

CHAPTER THREE: Traveler
p. 41, "He knew the Mississippi . . ." Long, *Mark Twain Handbook*, 109.
p. 41, "My life as a pilot . . ." Paul Fatout, *Mark Twain Speaking* (Iowa City: University of Iowa Press, 1976), 294.
p. 42, "that all war must be killing . . ." Mark Twain, "The Private History of a Campaign That Failed," *The American Claimant and Other Stories and*

Sketches (New York: P. F. Collier & Son Company, 1924),
278-279.

p. 43, "I never have *once* thought . . ." Albert Bigelow
Paine, *Mark Twain's Letters*, (New York: Harper &
Brothers Publishers, 1917), 1:85.

p. 44, "My starboard leg . . ." Paine, *Mark Twain*, 205.

p. 44, "My name is Clemens . . ." Ibid.

p. 47, "it was fearful drudgery . . ." Ferguson, *Mark Twain:
Man and Legend*, 96.

p. 49, "Coleman with his jumping frog . . ." Mark Twain,
Mark Twain's Notebook, ed. Albert Bigelow Paine
(Harper & Brothers Publishers, 1935), 7.

p. 51, "I don't see no . . ." Charles Neider, ed., "The Notorious
Jumping Frog of Calaveras County," *The Complete
Short Stories of Mark Twain* (New York: Bantam
Books, 1950), 1.

p. 51, "a villainous backwoods . . ." Ferguson, *Mark Twain:
Man and Legend*, 105.

p. 52, "oasis of golden memory . . ." Long, *Mark
Twain Handbook*, 138.

p. 53, "Home again, No . . ." Frederick Anderson,
Michael B. Frank, and Kenneth M. Sanderson, eds.,
Mark Twain's Notebooks & Journals (Berkeley: University
of California Press, 1975), 1:163.

p. 55, "Capt. Ned Blakely . . ." Mark Twain, *Roughing
It* (Hartford, CT: American Publishing Company,
1872), 352.

p. 57, "Do you wonder . . ." Justin Kaplan, *Mr. Clemens
and Mark Twain: A Biography* (New York: Simon &
Schuster, 1966), 54.

p. 57, "The ship is lying . . ." Twain, *Innocents
Abroad*, 222-223.

p. 58, "Thought we never . . ." Anderson, Frank, and
Sanderson, *Mark Twain's Notebooks & Journals*, 1: 432.

p. 59, "funeral excursion without . . ." Daniel Morley

McKeithan, ed., *Traveling with the Innocents Abroad* (Norman, OK: University of Oklahoma Press, 1958), 314.

p. 59-60, "Every individual . . ." Twain and Warner, *The Gilded Age*, 178.

p. 61-62, "It is forty years . . ." Paine, *Mark Twain*, 1:353.

CHAPTER FOUR: Courtship and Marriage

p. 64, "I am desperately in love . . ." Webster, *Mark Twain: Business Man*, 101-102.

p. 66, "I think all my references . . ." Harriet Elinor Smith and Richard Bucci, eds., *Mark Twain's Letters* (Berkeley: University of California Press, 1990), 2:357.

p. 69, "Mr. Langdon, whenever . . ." Paine, *Mark Twain*, 1:396.

p. 70, "I often feel . . ." Victor Fischer and Michael B. Franks, eds., *Mark Twain's Letters* (Berkeley: University of California Press, 1995), 4:311.

p. 71, "Just as soon as ever . . ." Paine, *Mark Twain's Letters*, 1:186.

p. 71, "I was young and ignorant . . ." Twain, *Roughing It*, 19.

p. 72-73, "*Roughing It* is a volume . . ." Charles Dudley Warner, "Mark Twain's New Book," *Hartford Courant*, March 18, 1872, http://etext.lib.virginia.edu/railton/roughingit/rirev06.html.

p. 73, "We can fancy the reader . . ." William Dean Howells, *Atlantic Monthly*, June 1872, http://etext.lib.virginia.edu/railton/roughingit/rirev02.html.

p. 77, "I am leaving you . . ." Twain and Warner, *The Gilded Age*, 82.

p. 80, "What a virgin subject . . ." Ferguson, *Mark Twain: Man and Legend*, 177.

p. 80, "I finished reading . . ." Paine, *Mark Twain's Letters*, 1:266.

p. 80, "It is *not* a boy's book . . ."Ibid, 1:258.

p. 80, "Although my book . . ." Twain, *The Adventures of Tom Sawyer*, preface.

p. 82, "Most of the adventures . . ." Mark Twain, *The Adventures of Tom Sawyer* (Middletown, CT: Xerox Education Publications, 1983), preface.

p. 82, "Those who regard . . ." David E. E. Sloane, *Student Companion to Mark Twain* (Westport, CT: Greenwood Press, 2001), 64.

CHAPTER FIVE: Author and Investor

p. 85, "nearly all the people . . ." Fatout, *Mark Twain Speaking*, 97.

p. 85, "at last a chance . . ." Ibid.

p. 86, "I have to smoke . . ." Kaplan, *The Singular Mark Twain*, 221.

p. 90, "I couldn't get General Grant . . ." Ibid., 356.

p. 91, "Then there is the beefsteak . . ." Mark Twain. *A Tramp Abroad* (New York: Penguin Books, 1997), 366.

p. 91, "It's awful undermining . . ." Ibid., 187.

p. 91, "the unutterable joy . . ." Paine, *Mark Twain's Letters*, 1:376.

p. 93, "There is no danger . . ." William Dean Howells, *My Mark Twain: Reminiscences and Criticisms* (Baton Rouge: Louisiana State University Press, 1967), 111.

p. 94, "Edward VI and a little pauper . . ." Paine, *Mark Twain's Notebook*, 129.

p. 94-95, "Mark Twain has finally . . ." Kaplan, *Mr. Clemens and Mark Twain*, 240.

p. 96, "To those who have followed . . ." Paine, *Mark Twain*, 2: 717-718.

p. 96, "it is unquestionably . . ." Susy Clemens, *Papa: An Intimate Biography of Mark Twain* (Garden City, NY: Doubleday & Company, Inc., 1985), 106.

p. 98, "Now when I had mastered . . ." Twain, *Life on the Mississippi*, 48.

p. 98, "broad expanse of the river . . ." Ibid.

p. 98, "that we are going . . ." Ibid.

p. 98-99, "imparts a great deal of useful . . ." Powers, *Mark Twain: A Life*, 469.

p. 99, "So far as I know . . ." Ibid.

p. 99-100, "I shall certainly reread . . ." Louis J. Budd, "Mark Twain's Reputation" in *The Oxford Companion to Mark Twain*, by Gregg Camfield (New York: Oxford University Press, 2003), 500.

p. 100, "I shall like it . . ." Ferguson, *Mark Twain: Man and Legend*, 217.

p. 100-101, "Persons attempting to find . . ." Mark Twain, *Adventures of Huckleberry Finn* (New York: W. W. Norton and Company, 1977), 2.

p. 101, "Pap warn't in good humor . . ." Ibid., 25.

p. 101, "Mr. Clemens has made . . ." "Review of *Huckleberry Finn*" *Hartford Courant*, Feb. 20, 1885, http://etext.virginia.edu/twain/harcour2.htm.

p. 102, "rough, coarse and inelegant, dealing with a series of experiences not elevating, the whole book being more suited to the slums than to intelligent, respectable people," "*Huckleberry Finn* Barred Out," *Boston Evening Transcript,* March 17, 1885, http://etext.virginia.edu/twain/boseven.html.

p. 102, "If Mr. Clemens cannot think . . ." Kaplan, *Mr. Clemens and Mark Twain*, 268.

p. 102, "The public library committee of Concord . . ." *Hartford Courant*, March 18, 1885, http://etext.virginia.edu/twain/hartcour.html

p. 103, "It's the best book . . ." Ernest Hemingway, *Green Hills of Africa* (New York: Macmillan Publishing Company, 1935), 22.

CHAPTER SIX: Financial Struggles

p. 108, "Mamma and I have both . . ." Clemens, *Papa*, 187.

p. 108, "Dream of being a knight . . ." Paine, *Mark Twain's Notebook*, 171.

p. 112, "Dear, dear sweetheart . . ." Dixon Wecter, ed., *The Love Letters of Mark Twain* (New York: Harper & Brothers, 1949), 344.

p. 112, "myriads have believed . . ." Ibid.

p. 113, "It's charming, original . . ." Henry Nash Smith and William M. Gibson, eds., *Mark Twain-Howells Letters* (Cambridge, MA: The Belknap Press, 1960), 612.

p. 113, "Well, my book is written . . ." Paine, *Mark Twain's Letters*, 2:514.

p. 114, "Merry Christmas to you . . ." Paine, *Mark Twain*, 2:901.

p. 115, "I might have known . . ." Smith and Gibson, *Mark Twain-Howells Letters*, 439.

p. 115, "We all regarded this break . . ." Kaplan, *The Singular Mark Twain*, 454.

p. 116, "What a talker he is . . ." Paine, *Mark Twain's Notebook*, 232.

p. 118, "We were strangers . . ." Twain, *Autobiography*, 1:256.

p. 120, "I've finished that book . . ." "Pudd'nhead Wilson and Those Extraordinary Twins" in Camfield, *The Oxford Companion to Mark Twain*, 465.

p. 120, "I mean to ship . . ." Ibid., 464.

p. 120, "I and mine, who were paupers . . ." Wecter, *The Love Letters of Mark Twain*, 292.

p. 121, "Certainly it [the typesetter] . . ." Paine, *Mark Twain*, 2:991.

CHAPTER SEVEN: Troubling Times

p. 123, "morally . . . one of the most honest . . ." Malcolm Bradbury, "Introduction," in *Puddn'head Wilson* by Mark Twain (New York: Penguin Books, 1986), 17.

p. 123, "the story at times rambles . . ." "Pudd'nhead Wilson and Those Extraordinary Twins," in Camfield,

The Oxford Companion to Mark Twain, 468.

p. 123, "Apparently, I've *got* to mount . . ." Lewis Leary, ed. *Mark Twain's Correspondence with Henry Huttleson Rogers* (Berkeley: University of California, 1969), 129.

p. 124, "To-night Joan was burned . . ." Paine, *Mark Twain*, 2:997.

p. 124, "Possibly the book may . . ." Ibid., 998.

p. 127-128, "I am not all troubled . . ." Howells, *My Mark Twain*, 131-132, 135.

p. 128, "Mark Twain as a historical . . ." Powers, *Mark Twain: A Life*, 522.

p. 128, "I like the *Joan of Arc* . . ." Paine, *Mark Twain*, 2:1034.

p. 128, "MARK TWAIN'S . . ." Kaplan, *The Singular Mark Twain*, 534.

p. 129, "I did know that Susy . . ." Paine, *Mark Twain's Letters*, 2:641.

p. 130, "The report of my illness . . ." Paine, *Mark Twain's Notebook*, 328.

p. 132, "*Adam was but human . . .*" Twain, *Puddn'head Wilson*, 61.

p. 134, "If we ever enter . . ." Paine, *Mark Twain*, 2:1112.

p. 134, "Something everybody wants . . ." Long, *Mark Twain Handbook*, 232.

p. 136, "Almost every tombstone . . ." DeVoto, *Mark Twain in Eruption*, 201.

p. 138, "put her arms around his neck . . ." Resa Willis, *Mark and Livy* (New York: Atheneum Publishers, 1992), 6.

p. 139, "How sweet she was . . ." Paine, *Mark Twain*, 3:1218.

p. 139, "I am tired & old . . ." Smith and Gibson, *Mark Twain-Howells Letters*, 785.

p. 139, "Got sei dir . . ." Paine, *Mark Twain*, 3:1223.

CHAPTER EIGHT: Halley's Comet Comes Again
p. 141, "there is no God . . ." Twain, "The Mysterious

Stranger" in *The Complete Short Stories of Mark Twain*, 679.

p. 144-145, "Why don't you ask why . . ." "Mark Twain in White Amuses Congressmen," *New York Times*, December 8, 1906, http://etext.virginia.edu/railton/sc_as_mt/suitnyt.html.

p. 146, "my don'tcareadam" Kaplan, *Mr. Clemens and Mark Twain*, 380.

p. 146, "It is a perfect house . . ." Paine, *Mark Twain*, 3:1450.

p. 148, "At last, you dear little . . ." John Cooley, ed., *Mark Twain's Aquarium: The Samuel Clemens Angelfish Correspondence* (Athens: The University of Georgia Press, 1991), 56-57.

p. 149, "I have been watching . . ." Ibid., 78.

p. 150, "Notice to the next burglar . . ." Paine, *Mark Twain*, 3:1463.

p. 150, "Dear child, you will be . . ." Kaplan, *The Singular Mark Twain*, 646.

p. 151, "a liar, a forger . . ." Kaplan, *Mr. Clemens and Mark Twain*, 386.

p. 151, "I came in with Halley's . . ." Paine, *Mark Twain*, 3:1511.

p. 151-152, "Yes, fully as much as . . ." Ibid., 1524.

p. 152, "Each event has its own . . ." DeVoto, *Mark Twain in Eruption*, 386.

p. 153, "I hear the newspapers . . ." Paine, *Mark Twain*, 3:1549.

p. 154, "Goodbye dear, if we . . ." Ferguson, *Mark Twain: Man and Legend*, 325.

p. 154, "I looked a moment . . ." Meltzer, *Mark Twain Himself*, 289.

p. 154, "Clemens was sole, incomparable . . ." Ibid.

Bibliography

Anderson, Frederick, Michael B. Frank, and Kenneth
   M. Sanderson. *Mark Twain's Notebooks & Journals*, Vol.
   1. Berkeley: University of California Press, 1975.
Camfield, Gregg. *The Oxford Companion to Mark Twain*.
   New York: Oxford University Press, 2003.
Clemens, Susy. *Papa: An Intimate Biography*. Garden City,
   NY: Doubleday & Company, Inc., 1985.
Cooley, John, ed. *Mark Twain's Aquarium: The Samuel
   Clemens Angelfish Correspondence*. Athens: The
   University of Georgia Press, 1991.
DeVoto, Bernard, ed. *Mark Twain in Eruption*. New
   York: Grosset & Dunlap, Publishers, 1940.
Fatout, Paul, ed. *Mark Twain Speaking*. Iowa City: University
   of Iowa Press, 1976.
Ferguson, DeLancey. *Mark Twain: Man and Legend*. New
   York: The Bobbs-Merrill Company, Inc., 1963.
Fischer, Victor, and Michael B. Frank, eds. *Mark Twain's
   Letters*, Vol. 4. Berkeley: University of California
   Press, 1995.
Hemingway, Ernest. *Green Hills of Africa*. New York:
   Macmillan Publishing Company, 1935.
Howells, William Dean. *My Mark Twain: Reminiscences
   and Criticisms*. Baton Rouge: Louisiana State
   University Press, 1967.
Kaplan, Fred. *The Singular Mark Twain*. New York:
   Doubleday, 2003.
Kaplan, Justin. *Mr. Clemens and Mark Twain: A Biography*.
   New York: Simon & Schuster, 1966.
Leary, Lewis, ed. *Mark Twain's Correspondence with Henry
   Huttleson Rogers*. Berkeley: University of California, 1969.
Long, E. Hudson. *Mark Twain Handbook*. New York: Hendricks
   House, 1957.
"Mark Twain in White Amuses Congressmen." *New York
   Times*, December 8, 1906. http://etext.virginia.edu/

railton/sc_as_mt/suitnyt.html.

McKeithan, Daniel Morley. *Traveling with the Innocents Abroad.* Norman, OK: University of Oklahoma Press, 1958.

Meltzer, Milton. *Mark Twain Himself.* New York: Wings Books, 1993.

Neider, Charles, ed. *The Complete Short Stories of Mark Twain.* New York: Bantam Books, 1990.

Paine, Albert Bigelow. *Mark Twain.* 3 vols. New York: Chelsea House, 1980.

———, ed. *Mark Twain's Letters.* 2 vols. New York: Harper & Brothers Publishers, 1917.

———. *Mark Twain's Notebook.* New York: Harper & Brothers Publishers, 1935.

Powers, Ron. *Mark Twain: A Life.* New York: Free Press, 2005.

Sloane, David E. E. *Student Companion to Mark Twain.* Westport, CT: Greenwood Press, 2001.

Smith, Harriet Elinor, and Richard Bucci. *Mark Twain's Letters*, Vol. 2. Berkeley: University of California Press, 1990.

Smith, Henry Nash, and William M. Gibson, eds. *Mark Twain-Howells Letters.* Cambridge, MA: The Belknap Press, 1960.

Twain, Mark. *The Adventures of Huckleberry Finn.* New York: W. W. Norton and Company, 1977.

———. *The Adventures of Tom Sawyer.* Middletown, CT: Xerox Education Publications, 1983.

———. *The American Claimant and Other Stories and Sketches.* New York: P. F. Collier & Son Company, 1924.

———. *The Innocents Abroad or The New Pilgrims Progress.* New York: New American Library, 1966.

———. *Life on the Mississippi.* New York: Bantam Books, 1981.

———. *Mark Twain's Autobiography.* 2 vols. New York: P. F. Collier and Son and Company, 1925.

———. *Puddn'head Wilson and Those Extraordinary Twins.* New York: Penguin Books, 1986.

———. *Roughing It*. Hartford, CT: American Publishing Company, 1872.

———. *1601, and Is Shakespeare Dead?* New York: Oxford University Press, 1996.

———. *A Tramp Abroad*. New York: Penguin Books, 1997.

———, and Charles Dudley Warner. *The Gilded Age: A Tale of Today*. New York: A Meridian Book, 1994.

Wagenknecht, Edward. *Mark Twain: The Man and His Work*. 3rd ed. Norman, OK: University of Oklahoma Press, 1967.

Warner, Charles Dudley. "Mark Twain's New Book." *Hartford Courant*, March 18, 1872. http://etext.lib.virginia.edu/railton/roughingit/rirev06.html.

Webster, Samuel Charles. *Mark Twain: Business Man*. Boston: Little, Brown and Company, 1946.

Wecter, Dixon, ed. *The Love Letters of Mark Twain*. New York: Harper & Brothers, 1949.

———. *Sam Clemens of Hannibal*. Cambridge, MA: The Riverside Press, 1952.

Willis, Resa. *Mark and Livy*. New York: Atheneum Publishers, 1992.

Web sites

http://www.marktwainhouse.org/
The Mark Twain House and Museum are featured on this site and includes information about the man, his Connecticut house, and a virtual tour of the museum.

http://www.gutenberg.org/browse/authors/t#a53
The Adventures of Huckleberry Finn, *The Adventures of Tom Sawyer*, *The Guilded Age*, *The Innocents Abroad*, *The Prince and the Pauper*, and *Life on the Mississippi* are among the many works by Twain that the Project Gutenberg Literary Archive Foundation has made freely available to the public to read online or download.

http://www.cmgworldwide.com/historical/twain
If you're searching for fast facts about Twain, general information about his writings, or want to browse a photo gallery that features a selection of different poses of Twain, this is the site to visit. Free desktop wallpaper and screen savers are available here, too.

http://www.twainquotes.com/
This searchable site is more than just quotes. Here you'll find newspaper and magazine articles written by Twain, special features, and links to a dozens of other sites, particularly university sites highlighting the life and times of Twain.

Index

Alcott, Louisa May, 102
Ament, Joseph P., 30

Beecher, Henry Ward, 55, *56*
Bell, Alexander Graham, 96
Bixby, Horace, 38-39, 41, 96
Blackmer, Margaret, 146
Blankenship, Tom, 27
Bliss, Elisha Jr., 60, 62, 74, 77
Bowen, Will, 19-20, 26, 81
Brown, William, 39
Burlingame, Anson, 53

Cable, G. W., 108, *109*
Clapp, Henry, 49
Clark, Charles Heber, 113
Clemens, Benjamin (brother),
    15, 17, 22, 75
Clemens, Clara (daughter),
    78, *94*, 95, *99*, 109, 115,
    123-124, 128, 132-133, *135*,
    136-137, 140, 146, 149-
    152, 154
Clemens, Henry (brother), 1
    7, 28, 31, 37, 39-40,
    66, 136
Clemens, Jane Lampton
    (mother), 11-19, 22-24, 26,
    28-30, 36-37, 43, 79, 81,
    109, 113-114, 136
Clemens, Jane Lampton
    "Jean" (daughter), 93, *94*,
    97, *99*, 109, 114-116, 123-
    124, 128, 130, 132-134,
    137, 140, 143, 149-151,
    153-154
Clemens, John Marshall

(father), 11-17, 20, 22-24,
    26-28, 40, 77, 81, 111, 136
Clemens, Langdon (son),
    69-70, 72, 74-75, 154
Clemens, Margaret (sister),
    15, 17
Clemens, Orion (brother),
    14, 16-17, 24, 28, 31, 34-
    37, 43, 54, 70, 74, 97,
    132, 152
Clemens, Pamela (sister),
    15, 17, 28, 33-35, 43,
    79, 140
Clemens, Pleasant Hannibal
    (brother), 15
Clemens, Samuel Langhorne,
    (see Mark Twain)
Clemens, Susan (daughter), 75,
    77, *94*, 95-96, *99*, 108-109,
    115-116, 123-124, 128-130,
    134, 153-154
Croker, Richard, 136, *136*

Daggett, Rollen, 95

Emerson, Ralph Waldo, 87-
    88, 90

Gabrilowitsch, Ossip, 133,
    151-152, 154
Garfield, James A., 95
Gillis, Steve, 46-48
Goodman, Joe, 46, 66, 96
Grant, Ulysses S., 29, 76-77,
    90, 104-108, *105*
Greely, Horace, 76

Hall, Frederick, 111, 114, 118

Harte, Bret, 47

Hayes, Rutherford B., 85-
86, *85*

Hemingway, Ernest, 103

Holmes, Oliver Wendell, 87-
88, *88*, 90

Horr, Elizabeth, 18-19

Howells, John Mead, 144

Howells, William Dean, 73,
79-80, 91, 93, 99, 112,
125, 127, *127*, 134, 139,
144, 154

Joan of Arc, 31, *32*, 116, 123

Keller, Helen, 130, *131*

Laffan, William, 115

Laird, James, 46

Langdon, Charles, 56, 61,
64, 95

Langdon, Jervis, 61, 63-
66, 68-69

Langdon, Olivia "Livy" (wife),
56, 61, 63-70, *64*, 74-75,
77-80, 97, *99*, 111-112, 115,
122-124, 128-129, 134,
135, 136-140, 153-154

Leary, Katy, 95, 115, 124,
128, 137-140, 143, 153-154

Lincoln, Abraham, 42-43

Longfellow, Henry Wadsworth,
87-88, 90

Lyon, Isabel, 137-138,
146, 149-151

Moffett, William, 35, 39

Nast, Thomas, 76

Osgood, James R., 95, 98, 104

Paige, James W., 111-112,
114, 116, 122

Paine, Alfred Bigelow, 142-
143, *143*, 150, 153

Pope Leo XIII, 107-108, *107*

Potter ,Edward, 78

Quarles, John (uncle), 15-
16, 20

Quarles, Patsy (aunt), 15

Rees, George, 37

Rogers, Henry Huttleston,
118, *119*, 120-121, 122-
124, 130, 138, 142, 149, 151

Sherman, William Tecumseh,
55

Stewart, William, 59, *60*

Stowe, Harriet Beecher, 72

Tilden, Samuel J., 85

Twain, Mark, *10*, *33*, *61*, *65*,
68, *76*, *92*, *99*, *109*, *125*,
129, *135*, *142*, *143*, *144*, *145*
147

Birth, 12

Birth of daughter Clara, 78

Birth of daughter Jean, 93

Birth of daughter Susan, 75

Birth of son Langdon, 69

Death, 154

Death of brother Benjamin, 22
Death of brother Henry, 40
Death of daughter Jean, 153
Death of daughter Susan, 128
Death of father, 27
Death of mother, 114
Death of son Langdon, 75
Death of wife Olivia, 139
First usage of penname Mark Twain, 44
First writing job, 31
Marriage to Olivia Langdon, 67
Works,
    A Connecticut Yankee in King Arthur's Court, 108, 110-113, *110*
    A Tramp Abroad, 89-91
    "Captain Stormfield's Visit to Heaven," 146
    Following the Equator: A Journey Around the World, 132
    Innocents Abroad, 19-20, 27, 57, 62, 63, 66, 74, 93
    Life on the Mississippi, 83, 88, 97-100
    Personal Recollections of Joan of Arc, 31, 124-125, *126*, 127-128
    Pudd'nhead Wilson, 117-118, *117*, 120, 122
    Roughing It, 55, 70, 72-75

    The Adventures of Huckleberry Finn, 83, 88, 93, 100-103, 104, 118
    The Adventures of Tom Sawyer, 24, 78-82, *81*, 83, 88, 100, 118
    "The Celebrated Jumping Frog of Calaveras County," 49, 51
    The Gilded Age, 15, 59-60, 77
    "The Man That Corrupted Hadleyburg," 133
    "The Mysterious Stranger," 141
    "The Turning Point of My Life," 152
    The Prince and the Pauper, 90, 93, 95-96, 118
    Tom Sawyer Abroad, 116
Twichell, Joseph, 66-67, *67*, 72, 75, 80, 89, 129, 139, 151

Wakemen, Edgar, 54-55
Ward, Artemus, 49
Warner, Charles Dudley, 72-73, *73*, 77
Webster, Charles, 104, 111
Whittier, John Greenleaf, 86, *87*, 90